W9-CQB-751

dematerializing

Jane Hammerslough

dematerializing

Taming the Power of
POSSESSIONS

PERSEUS PUBLISHING

Cambridge, Massachusetts

A CIP record for this book is available from the Library of Congress.

ISBN: 0-7382-0386-6

Printed in the United States of America.

Perseus Publishing is a member of the Perseus Books Group.

Perseus Publishing books are available at special discounts for bulk purchases in the U.S. by corporations, institutions, and other organizations. For more information, please contact the Special Markets Department at the Perseus Books Group, 11 Cambridge Center, Cambridge, MA 02142, or call (617) 252-5298.

Visit us on the World Wide Web at http://www.perseuspublishing.com

Text design by Jeffrey P. Williams
Set in 11.5-point New Caledonia by Perseus Publishing Services

First printing, August 2001

1 2 3 4 5 6 7 8 9 10—03 02 01

For Ezra

Contents

⁘

⁘

Acknowledgments

The idea for this book began in an elementary school hallway, and began to grow on a bunch of playgrounds, in several college classrooms and libraries, and across innumerable kitchen tables, telephone lines, and Internet connections. I couldn't have written it without the help of a lot of generous people.

I'd like to thank Alison Hendrie, Kathy Gabbay, Rachel Wallach, Lisa Benton, Kimberly Lake, Diane Kolyer, Jonathan Wagner, Suzy Berne, Peter Blauner, Peg Tyre, Deborah Barnett-Brandt, Stacy Prince, Betsey Lebow, Debra Koenig, Reid Rosefelt, Peter and Louisa Palmer, Maggie Kneip, John Hammerslough, Charles and Colleen Hammerslough, Hank Weisinger, Susan Mason, Fred Stern, Elizabeth Broad, Kathy Wheeler, and Linda Floch who gave their time, energy, and support to this project. Thanks also to the many friends, acquaintances, and students who shared their stories with me.

I owe a special debt of gratitude to Nancy Hammerslough and Donna Haupt, tireless readers who provided help, humor and support from the start—and all along the way. Both my agent, Andrew Blauner, and Marnie Cochran, my editor at

Perseus Books, offered encouragement and wise advice, along with a lot of laughs. I'm very grateful to all of them.

Finally, and especially, I'd like to thank Ezra, Phineas, and Zachariah Palmer, for helping me so much in writing this book. Again and again, they provided insight, comic relief, and boundless support and enthusiasm—and gave me the reason to start asking the questions.

1

࿓

MATERIALIZING

The world is too much with us; late and soon,
Getting and spending, we lay waste our powers. . .

—WILLIAM WORDSWORTH,
"THE WORLD IS TOO MUCH WITH US"

At my son's back-to-school night, I studied the smiling self-portraits of second-graders hung in the hallway under the bulletin-board banner asking, "Who Am I?" Our challenge as parents that evening was to find our own children among the sea of colorful, unsigned faces. To help, each portrait had a carefully printed description of its creator stapled to the bottom.

One child wrote that he liked dinosaurs and soccer, and hated cleaning up his room. Another said that she had a new bike, a baby sister, and coyly mentioned that her best friend's name began with a "B." Another noted that he was tall, had green eyes, and liked science and his cat. And one of the pieces of writing stood out, not for what it said, but for what it didn't.

The essay began with "I have . . ." and a long list of things followed: a new video-game system, a signed celebrity photograph, coin and card collections, and a television, among other

1

items. There wasn't a word about what the child did or didn't like, no mention of doing sports or music or reading or art. It didn't include anything about friends, or family, or even pets.

Of course, all kids sometimes get the "gimmes," or get obsessed with their toys or the latest collecting fad at school. But surely there was something else the child could say to describe himself. What kind of materialistic values was he learning, anyway?, I thought, smug with the knowledge that my own child was the tall one interested in science. For the other young writer, "who I am" was simply a summary of what he owned. It struck me as sad and strange.

And, I'll admit, a bit unnerving. As I stood in the school hallway, that little essay made something go off in my head. And I didn't like what I was hearing.

That kid wasn't the only one living in the place where "who I am" and "what I have" meet. Frankly, my own feelings about wanting, buying, and owning objects at the time were making me increasingly uneasy. Like my inability to see a house, while on vacation, without wanting to own it. Or my worrying that my kids would fall behind their classmates if I didn't get some new CD-ROM or another. Or my near-obsessive, months-long search for the right couch for our family room.

What me, materialistic? I'd never seen myself that way. But there I was, pricing waterfront property instead of enjoying the view, agonizing about depriving my kids instead of noticing the pile of unused CD-ROMs they already owned, and sweating over fabric swatches for a fantasy family room—instead of spending the time actually doing something with my family. If I wasn't materialistic, I sure was giving a lot of thought and meaning to material things. And I was beginning to find that my expectations of objects to *do* something—as well as the time and energy I was devoting to them—wasn't giving me what I wanted.

Okay, we live in a material world, and the stuff we own matters. That doesn't necessarily make us materialistic, but what we drive, where we live, and what we wear, collect, or covet can all have meaning. After all, possessions can make our lives easier, give aesthetic pleasure, offer a certain amount of security, deliver a message to other people, and sometimes even deliver on the promise of providing hours of fun. And given the current climate of consumption where messages linking ownership with identity are louder than ever, the power in possessions isn't lost on anyone. Not on me, and not even on a seven-year-old. Or perhaps, especially not on a seven-year-old.

So what's wrong with this picture? I knew that I wasn't thrilled with the ever-expanding space that objects seemed to be occupying in my life and in my thoughts, and I wanted some fast answers. To try to get a handle on the issue, I started asking questions: First off, did anyone else feel the same way?

I found, overwhelmingly, that I wasn't alone. Plenty was wrong with the current picture; 95 percent of Americans said most of us are "very materialistic," and more than 85 percent believe that young people are far too preoccupied with owning and consuming things, according to a Merck Family Fund study. And the people that I started grilling on the subject agreed that materialism increasingly dominates our lives and may undermine our most important values. From my colleagues and professional contacts in my work as a newspaper and magazine writer to fellow teachers and students at the college where I was teaching English, from total strangers to close friends, the widespread concern—not just for ourselves, but for our kids and the future—became clear. But it's also complex. Objects are important, no doubt. But at what price?

That honest, anonymous elementary-school essay had taken the importance of objects to a troubling extreme, as if owning and being are one and the same. Possessions don't entirely fill "who I am" for most people, but they naturally occupy space as part of "self." Let's face it: It's fun to buy a pair of new shoes sometimes. It's a pleasure to get the car you've coveted for a while. And there's nothing like that look on a child's face when she opens your gift and it's just what she'd hoped for. Objects can, at times, make us happy. But ultimately, do they give us what we really want?

And that's where things started getting tricky. Possessions have meaning, and always have and always will. So I began to consider the issue from another angle: Not whether objects themselves are good or bad, but how and why the faith we place in ownership may intrude on what we want most.

I started by looking backward. This isn't the first time anyone has questioned how the importance of "stuff" affects other areas of our lives, and it seemed to make sense that our current state of materialism might have grown out of the ancient idea of materializing. Materializing is a basic element of age-old myth and miracles, when the spirit of something becomes real and tangible. In the spirit of goodness, manna appeared in the desert to save the starving. Loaves and fishes multiplied to feed the hungry. A genie appeared at the hour of need to grant wishes.

And in the tradition of materializing, we've had countless stories of transformation, where something bad turns good, and something good gets better. A fairy godmother appears, and Cinderella's rags become a ball gown, a pumpkin turns into a coach, and mice become coachmen. The frog turns into a prince, the small snake in an African folktale becomes a king.

As a result of great faith or good acts, miracles and miraculous changes occur, taking earthly shape in what's needed or desired. Our fables illustrate fulfillment of especially unlikely possibility, capturing the moment when hope becomes reality. The proof of that power takes form in something we can see and touch.

Magic? Perhaps. There's power in thought and deed, and magic moves in mysterious ways, both in the old stories and in real life. And if magic manifests itself in something tangible, well then, isn't the object magical, too?

Magic is a mixed bag in the old stories. Take the red shoes in Hans Christian Andersen's fairy tale: The shoes enable their wearer, a girl named Karen, to realize her dream to dance. But once she begins to dance she can't stop—and she can't remove the shoes, either. In the end, she's finally forced to forego her feet (a helpful woodcutter takes care of the job) in order to achieve some peace.

It's a grisly and ominous conclusion. And while it's unlikely that this morality tale plays out to such an extreme in our own lives—sure, we could point fingers at Imelda Marcos or Leona Helmsley, but it *is* a fairy tale, after all—the story points up the ambiguous nature of the power in possessions. Be careful what you wish for, it warns. Ownership can give you what you want, but there may be a hidden cost.

With further research, I began to realize that materialism is an issue that's not easily solved or summarized. Much as I tried to compartmentalize cause and effect, it didn't have a simple beginning, a middle, and an end. And as I began talking with people who might be "experts" on the subject—mental health pros, members of the clergy, and academics—along with reading ancient philosophers and more recent social commentators, the issue only got more complex.

But as I became more and more immersed in the subject, at least one thing started to become clearer to me: The problem of materialism encroaching on more important values, it seemed, was not just about getting (or not getting) the shoes or the car or the gift. And while recent, over-the-top consumption has created concern about new houses that look like hotels, landfills crowded with cast-off computers, and renewed discussion about the legacy of limited resources we may be leaving our grandchildren, worries about materialism dig in still deeper. Which led me to believe the question wasn't just about what is or isn't excessive. The deeper issue is the power we seek from possessions, and its repercussions on other areas of our lives.

That power appears, like the manna in the desert, with faith. Faith that the new shoes may be the key to getting the cute guy to take notice, or that they are the way to get over a lousy day at a dead-end job you should have left long ago, or that owning them will somehow alleviate boredom with the rest of your life.

Faith that the new car is the answer to the nagging sense of feeling older and undesirable, or that it will keep you safe from all those crazy drivers out there, or that it will finally show your snotty neighbor just how successful you really are.

Faith that the gift to your child will atone for a lack of time and energy in the past, or that it will help make him brighter, or that it will somehow make it easier for the two of you to talk. Or faith, for example, that my fantasy family room (where, needless to say, nobody would ever fight, tattle, leave dirty socks, or spill grape juice) would play out in real life if I just got the right couch. Unlike the manna in the desert, however, this kind of faith doesn't just translate into the material good; it *is* the material good.

With faith in the power of possessions to answer deeper needs, the subject becomes the object. And the object becomes the answer.

Who doesn't want to believe in magic, in answers obtained with the flick of a credit card? Sure, a measure of belief in material things—that the new pair of shoes will fit, the car will run, the kid might like the gift, and it won't break immediately—is essential to functioning in the world. And like the small, bright flicker that emerged along with the evils out of Pandora's box, hope—that change is possible, that improvement is available, that pain has an end—is what can keep any of us going when times get tough. But when an object doesn't give you what you really need, what next?

The promise of possessions to fulfill a tangle of needs, wants, and desires is seductive, fast, and easy. But it also takes up space, not just in our closets, but in our lives. It takes up time. It takes up energy. And I found that for me, as well as for people who spoke with me about materialism in their own lives, it may not be enough:

I thought my kids would stop fighting over control of the TV when we bought another. Now they fight about who gets to watch the new TV.

I buy clothes and bring them home and when I look at them a few days later, they're always wrong. The size isn't quite right, or the color is off, or the style isn't really me. I buy things hoping to find what I'm looking for, but I always seem to end up feeling dissatisfied.

It seems like every time I go to a party these days, all anyone can talk about is what they just bought, or what they're planning to buy. I keep thinking back to when we were younger and all that stuff didn't seem to matter so much. Nobody seems to know how to have fun anymore.

My four-year-old can't pass by a thing without wanting it. And when he finally gets the toy, it's not what he thought it would be. Five minutes later he's demanding something else. All I seem to hear is 'I want, I want, I want.'

What *do* we want from ownership? And why does having what we want and wanting what we have seem so tough these days?

✿   ✿   ✿

At various times throughout history, the belief that "the world is too much with us" has prompted people to retreat to a kind of life that seems simpler, more elemental, less concerned with "getting and spending." This sort of quest has usually meant checking out of an environment of materialism, from ancient ascetics seeking solitary insight, to Henry David Thoreau's spending time in a modest cabin to write *Walden*, to more recent movements of people heading "back to the land."

For most of us, however, chucking it all for a "simple" life in the woods isn't an option. For many reasons, not the least of which is the current price of real estate (just imagine what Thoreau's little Massachusetts cabin and waterfront land would go for now!) and a pesky lack of independent income, taking off isn't the answer. And even if money is no object, an understandable fondness for, say, indoor plumbing as well as a reasonable desire to interact with other people gets in the way. For better or worse, most of us must make do with living and working in the real world.

Which is now filled with enough messages on the benefits of getting and spending to make Thoreau's—or one's own—head spin. Every day, we receive upwards of 3,000 marketing messages. Someone, somewhere, may be able to exist without exposure to television, the Internet, radio, newspapers, magazines, and billboards, but for most people checking out and shutting down isn't a choice—or even desirable. And although we might be able to avoid pounds of catalogues and junk mail, or dodge phone calls during dinner from someone trying to sell something, for many of us, it's part of a regular reality. Engaging in modern life means living with a barrage of information on things to buy.

And why not? After all, we live in a world that focuses on getting and spending, creating and selling. And through it all, millions of people support their families, putting a roof over their heads and food on the table by contributing to the process. While those hiding out in the woods might eloquently disparage this reality (although even Thoreau, during the two years in his simple cabin, made regular trips out to town for meals and companionship), there's not a whole lot anyone can do about it. And while we could endlessly debate whether the vast volume of messages that we now receive are morally reprehensible or useful, necessary tools, there's no question that they simply *are.*

It doesn't take a marketing genius to understand the premise of dissatisfaction uniting the voices and images in all those messages: You've got a problem, and there is a purchasable solution. Something is inadequate and needs to be fixed, improved, or, better yet, replaced. Something is scary or dangerous, and needs to be controlled. Something is missing and the hole it's left in your life needs to be filled.

A lot has been said about the evils of advertising and its supposedly subliminal messages that glorify greed and violence and promise everything from fabulous sex to stellar athletic performance. And much has been made of sales pitches that undermine everything from family values to family finances. Been there, done that. The bottom line is this: Like it or not, it's still part of the scenery.

Within that scenery are some old stories. Messages for breath mints or perfume echo legends of magic potions and eternal love. The tale of King Midas, whose touch turned everything to gold, appears in the pitch for furniture polish or a software program. Villains and heroes, magic and miracles abound, but in the modern retelling, the nasty bits are cut out. We don't hear that the potion that may have guaranteed eternal love also meant eternal sleep, or that Midas's magic power also meant that his daughter turned to gold like everything else. Like the perfect fit of the glass slipper in the fairy tale, there's a problem, and the answer lies in the promise of transformation: Acquiring something magically eliminates your troubles. Mastering possibilities becomes a matter of using a credit card.

But let's get real here. Do we truly believe that the flawless face of the fourteen-year-old model will become ours with the purchase of the right moisturizer? That drinking one kind of beer over another is the answer to loneliness? That using a particular dishwasher detergent will make your mother-in-law admire you? Or that installing the right brand of cabinets will be enough to bring folks together for cozy chats in the kitchen?

Of course not. We don't blindly buy into the messages of marketers, eager for a sale. But there's no question that the volume of words and images telling stories of miraculous change—and oh, so easily had!—are greater than ever before. And the human desire—for everlasting love, the security of riches, or whatever else we might wish for—remains.

All that external wisdom floating around can strike a complex, internal chord of desire when we least expect it. And while we may not wholeheartedly, simple-mindedly embrace the one-note, purchasable solution to meet that desire, we can't help but hear it.

You hear that the fast-food meal is no longer just a hamburger and fries—it's the break you need today. You hear that the athletic gear, endorsed by a sports superstar, is imbued with the talent of champions. You hear that the brand of bourbon you drink is a way to communicate something positive about the sort of person you are, or wish to be. Over and over again, you hear it, you see it, and maybe you even start to feel it. It's not a straight shot from acquisition to experience, from ownership to identity, but through sheer volume and repetition, a path gets forged.

What's Changed?

The spiritual, emotional, and social significance of objects is nothing new. For thousands of years, people have put their faith in objects, from amulets to icons, to control the unknown, offer protection from evil or misfortune, and bring good luck. Long before this vast amount of information on problems and material solutions existed, ownership and display of objects has been a way to communicate power, status, and wealth. What's different these days is how acutely we may feel the downside of placing faith in possessions—and the impact of the power of acquisition and ownership on the way we live, connect to others, and view ourselves. Where do we draw the line on that faith?

The fact that we are now inundated with messages linking objects and the limitless gratification of desires is just part of what's contributed to the current climate of materialism. But what other factors make possessions so powerful these days? Several things may contribute:

The urgency of technology.   Basic needs such as food, shelter, and protection from dangerous elements haven't changed. However, as we have gained knowledge of and control over unknowns through technology, the concept of what we need to survive has grown. And not without reason: The accelerated pace of technological developments over the last three decades brings up new needs and different, possibly more efficient, solutions. Now, as in the past, survival may sometimes be a matter of possessing certain tools.

What's different now, however, is that today's frenetic pace involves an infinite, ever-changing variety of material solutions.

This idea hit home one day in the early 1990s when I ran into a neighbor on my block in Brooklyn. A kind, gentle man who was once a well-known musician, he had gotten involved with drugs, was convicted for robbery, and had spent the better part of the last decade in prison. Now he was out, clean and sober, and quickly getting back on track with his music. That day he was hauling a Selectric typewriter home, a perfectly good find from a discard pile on the street. "Look!" he said, his eyes lighting up. "This is a great machine. I know," he said, grinning, "because I used to steal them!"

Admiring his haul, I didn't have the heart to tell him that Selectrics were a dime a dozen on any given garbage day in our neighborhood at that time. Or that if he looked a bit more, he could probably even find an early, working PC and dot matrix printer. With my own mind occupied by whether I should have faster speed, laser printing, and other features that were then the latest in computer technology, my neighbor's delight in an old electric typewriter seemed a touching time warp.

To keep up with such speedy changes, we're forced to give material objects more thought. Solving problems we never knew about in the past has now become a pressing necessity.

Like the Luddites, the group of rebel British laborers in the early nineteenth century who destroyed textile-making machinery in hopes of preserving their jobs and way of life, we can rage against machines. But, as the Luddites soon discovered, the tide keeps coming in. Change occurs whether we want it or not; survival may depend on adapting to technology.

Just how much is uncertain. In recent years, rapid technological advances have resulted in more purchasable, problem-solving options than ever. Yet within the benefits of the new is a warning that works on a fear that's timeless: If you don't buy in now, you may be left behind, excluded, or even perish.

The increasing array of problems and products.   In the 1950s, supermarkets displayed about 3,000 items; today, they may stock upwards of 30,000. Every day, around thirty-four new food products alone are introduced. The dizzying array of new items reflects a microsplitting of problems to create more "must-have" new solutions.

Take toothpaste, for example. The choice there is no longer a matter of simply picking up one brand over another. It now means considering an ocean of answers to a whole host of problems, such as a debate between "oral health" vs sex appeal, or gel vs paste. And then there are still the troubles of tartar, plaque, gingivitis, and halitosis that need attacking. The decision becomes still more complicated when you throw in factors like whiteness, brightness, tastiness, and cool appearance, like sparkles or stripes in the stuff. Yikes!

All those options demand attention. Okay, so maybe you don't have an existential dilemma every time you're in the pharmacy aisle. But the sheer number of choices requires engaging, if only for a few seconds, in order to make a decision. Sure, the bits of thought and effort you expend are small, but they can add up. And the process starts all over again when you move to, say, the snacks section.

In the early days of automobiles, Henry Ford announced that a customer could have a Model T in any color he wanted— so long as it was black. It made the choice of choosing a car simpler, for sure. But since we're not about to go back to such a "take it or leave it" approach to buying cars (or for that matter, anything else), we've now got to deal with nearly limitless options. Obviously, we want choices; we ask for them. But the growing number of choices of material things demands more of us.

More products connecting the "spirit" of the subject with material objects.   The number of objects tied in to other subjects—from characters in books, on television, or in movies, to real-life sports stars and other celebrities—has exploded in recent years. Consider the Davy Crockett coonskin cap of the past against today's billion-dollar licensing business, which includes everything from food to bedsheets to plastic figures, each imbued with the essence of a character's experience.

A truly massive number of these items are available today. And because many are available for a "limited time only," their shelf life is ever-shortening: What's hot among the under-ten set this season is likely to end up in a dump within a couple of years, since something new is constantly coming along to supplant it. However, the phenomenon linking the spirit of something to a material object is hardly limited to the "each sold separately" array of toys or trading cards ("collect them all!") that plague parents. The number of ways to tap into the intangible has grown for grown-ups as well.

In the early 1990s, Sotheby's held an auction of the estate of Andy Warhol, the artist as much known for his prophesy that in the future, "everyone will be famous for fifteen minutes" as for his pop-art paintings. Like a giant tag sale, the auction of the artist's belongings included everything from furniture to paintings to his mammoth collection of old cookie jars—not rare ginger jars, but things he'd picked up at thrift shops. The surprise of the sale was how much the kitschy cookie jars commanded: People paid many hundreds of times what Warhol himself had spent, far more than what they might have paid had they found the same mass-produced product at a local church's tag sale. The fact that these were *Andy Warhol's* cookie jars, chosen and touched by an art superstar, made them intrinsically more valuable.

The Warhol auction—along with those of the late Jacqueline Kennedy Onassis, the Duchess of Windsor, Princess Diana, and lesser-known luminaries—demonstrates the current focus on how possessing a piece of private life, however remote, may provide a personal link to a public person. The fact that young John Kennedy was captured on film pulling on his mother's fake pearls when his father was in office pushed their sale price up to over $300,000. What sold the faux pearls and other items was not their inherent value (after all, for about fifty bucks, you could find a strand just like them almost anywhere) but the rare spirit of celebrity they contained: They were the *only ones* the First Lady actually wore in the photograph.

Even if you don't happen to be in the market for expensive stuff belonging to famous dead people, opportunities abound to buy things blessed by the essence of someone. Think of polo-playing Ralph's upscale items, cool Tommy's casual clothing, superstar Tiger's athletic wear, and tasteful Martha's home collections. With first-name familiarity, we can all have access to a bit of the magic, the success, the fame.

What comes first—the licensed product or the character or story which inspires it? What spawns what—the image of the creator or the object that's created? It's a chicken-and-egg issue these days. As opposed to, say, the twelfth century, when the bones of a saint or an alleged bit of the true cross became the object of pilgrimages, our current quests focus on that which is mass-produced. While reverence of relics is nothing new, the number of things linking ownership with the spirit of a person or an experience has grown dramatically.

Values: The new consumable good.   The word "value" comes from the Latin *valere*, meaning to be strong or to be worth. Modern definitions can include the material or monetary worth of something, the relative rank, importance, or usefulness of something, or that which has intrinsic worth. As a verb, it can also mean "to estimate" or "appraise," or "to esteem" or "find worthy." A good value can be something that doesn't cost too much for what it delivers or provides to its purchaser; it can also be something that's a source of strength, purchasable or not.

The many different definitions of "value" have increasingly become incorporated into consumption culture: A fairly low price and decent quality for an item are no longer the only standards of what makes for good "value." The other sense of value—a source of strength or esteem—creeps into material objects as well.

How? More than ever, we're asked to question our own values—the qualities we esteem most—in relation to purchasing something. Those questions may come from the ever-present external wisdom of advertisers. They may come from the judgments of our friends, coworkers, or even strangers. Or they may come from something inside ourselves. Whatever the source, the choice of a product may now imply a kind of moral decision that didn't exist in the distant past: Don't you care

enough to send the very best flowers? Don't you want to protect your kids most effectively from germs? Shouldn't that an-
niversary bauble say "you'd marry her all over again"?

In response, the onus of ownership grows. The decision to
buy something isn't simply just a way to get a little pleasure or
to make life a bit easier or more convenient—it has become a
crossroads. And the right choice may be equated with taking
some sort of moral high road. After all, who *doesn't* want to do
what's right for themselves, their friends, or their children?

If you can actually buy that kind of "righteousness," bully for
you. Then again, anyone knows that objects of desire can't really embody the subtleties, challenges, and hard work of up-
holding what we believe is most important. We know it's simpler—and certainly smarter—to keep the two types of values
separate, since rationally, we're aware that chance can toss a
curveball at any moment: No matter what diamond ring you
bestow, the relationship might fall apart. But sorting out various "values" isn't always so simple to do. And since there may
be more fear than ever of those unpredictable curveballs, we
hear about objects stepping up to the plate for us.

An advertisement for a brand of blue jeans brings this not-so-
subtle point home. In the six-page spread, a series of captioned
photographs chronicles the romances of several hip, young subjects, noting the length of each relationship: "Callie & Ty, three
years," "Callie and Noah, one year, five months." Turn the page,
and the luv do-si-do continues with other partners: Noah hooks
up with Kim, then Kim moves on to Jeremy, and Jeremy winds
up with Andrea. At least for now. The caption there tells us their
bliss has lasted for a full week and a half.

In the final photo, Andrea's hugging a friend in a kitchen somewhere. A poster that says "Mis Padres se Divorcian" appears in the background. Okay kids, put it together—your parents divorced and your own relationships begin and end like train wrecks? Never fear—jeans are here! With subtle nuances like that, we don't really need the caption that tells us, "At least some things last forever . . ." and identifies which brand to buy.

There's a strange, mixed-up cynicism here: You may want lasting love, but you'll have to settle for lasting jeans. The subtext is that if you buy the jeans, maybe love will endure, too.

Of course, it's only an advertisement. But it illustrates the current moral framework of materialism, which links intangible values with those you can buy. In this skewed framework, however, only some values are worth possessing; others, such as patience, forbearance, acceptance, compassion, modesty, thrift, and, uh, self-restraint, are notably absent.

Homogeneity über alles. Consider "Pied Beauty," Gerard Manley Hopkins's 1918 poem celebrating the beauty of diversity and the diversity of beauty. Hopkins praises the creator of "dappled things," "rose-moles all in a stipple upon trout that swim," "fresh-firecoal chestnut-falls," and "finches' wings," among other small delights:

> *All things counter, original, spare, strange;*
> *Whatever is fickle, freckled (who knows how?)*
> *With swift, slow, sweet, sour; adazzle, dim;*
> *He fathers-forth whose beauty is past change:*
> *Praise him.*

Hopkins's images of unique beauty in the ordinary and love-liness in the contrary have made the poem endure. But you have to wonder what the poet would make of the increasing fo-cus on homogeneity that defines beauty (or success, or desir-ability) these days. The exuberance of being naturally, beauti-fully "pied" and "past change" may have been fine once, but today, it's often about shuffling toward sameness—and the things we can buy to change ourselves to reach that ideal.

Fashions have always come and gone, from women coating themselves with deadly lead to look paler, to men wearing wigs and heels to help them look taller. The long-fickle nature of fashion might make you question whether a "pinup" of the past would be called a "bombshell" today—or just characterized as another overweight blonde with a pretty face. Fashion's foibles might even make you look at pictures of your younger self and shudder. (And not without reason, you might say.)

We've always darted between various standards of beauty. What's different today is the number of ways we learn about those exacting standards, and the quantity of products that can help us transform into that rigid standard ourselves.

Indeed, the stakes are higher. Celebration of conformity may have always been out there, but it's never had such a captive audience. Through more images than ever, we learn about in-creasingly unforgiving and finite ideals, from the way both men and women are supposed to look to the way success is defined. And it may extend beyond a sense of style into a sense of self.

In other words, it doesn't end with how you are supposed to look or what you are supposed to wear. That's just the starting point for who you're *supposed to be* at a certain point in life—about what you need to *own* to live that role. If you want to be a Cool Teen, an Ambitious Twenty-something, a Having-it-All Mom, a Respected Business Person, or an Active Senior (to name a few) there are props involved: Buy in or get lost.

Such strict, superficial definitions of what's desirable translate to an equally facile and narrow vision of success. Owning or consuming certain things makes you a winner. Not having them—you guessed right—means you're a loser.

Just because we hear it doesn't make it true, of course. But the other side of the story—beauty in the "strange," success in the heart—may be overshadowed by the ways we now hear about desirability that's anything but unique. Again and again and again.

New communities and the common language. At a recent Fourth of July celebration on a small island off the coast of New England, two people standing near me struck up a conversation about an old episode of *Friends*. Shouting to be heard over the live music, they ignored the kids on the jetty excitedly lighting Roman candles and the boats in the harbor loudly blowing their horns. By the time the fireworks started, the two friends moved on to a different episode of *Friends*, clearly no less intriguing to them than the booming spectacle overhead, since their discussion continued halfway through the magnificent display. Finally, they stopped talking about old reruns and turned their attention to the living color of the present. At the end, they loudly agreed that this year's show wasn't as good as the ones in the past.

All obnoxiousness aside, the conversation points up how the mass media may be greater than the sum of its parts, bringing people together by becoming the common language. That's not to say that the characters from TV's *Friends* move into our apartments and we confuse them with our real friends, but their weekly, fictional antics may provide an increasingly important point of reference among real people.

Meanwhile, the concept of "community" has grown, now encompassing both the news we hear at town hall and the news from faraway cities on TV, including the people we meet at church or synagogue and the people who share our interests in cyberspace. The common language of the mass media is spoken and understood by more people now than ever before. And that common language may influence how we define and relate to other people.

In *Amusing Ourselves to Death: Public Discourse in the Age of Show Business*, media ecologist Neil Postman writes that television "is our culture's principal mode of knowing about itself. Therefore. . . how television stages the world becomes the model for how the world is properly to be staged. It is not merely that on the television screen entertainment is the metaphor for all discourse. It is that off the screen the same metaphor prevails." These days, one might make that case for all "screens"—and throw in every other kind of consumer-driven communication while we're at it. How mass communication continually defines the haves and have-nots and discerns between those who can keep up and those who can't doesn't just influence what we need or want ourselves. It may cast a different, harsher light on how we judge or relate to other people.

And it may contribute to people feeling more pressured than ever to buy things. The idea of showing status through possessions is well established, existing long before Thorstein Veblen published *The Theory of the Leisure Class* in 1899. However, it was he who coined the terms "conspicuous consumption" and "conspicuous waste" to bitingly describe how ownership can announce accomplishment. And it was Veblen—an eccentric, perpetually broke, failed academic, nonetheless known for his great success with the ladies—who identified the importance of possessions in conveying personal "reputability" and "decency" to the world at large.

Jump ahead a hundred years or so and the ante has gone up considerably. The link between "decency"—acceptability and admiration from one's community, which may translate into self-respect—and consumption is bolstered, if not celebrated, by a breadth and volume of "communities" unimaginable in Veblen's day. Hey, the people in that TV show are just like you, and look at the amazing furnishings *they* have! The creepy guy in the movie drives an ancient, beat-up car—how embarrassing that your boyfriend's subcompact looks just like it! While thinking humans aren't in the habit of monkey-see, monkey-want, it's hard to avoid those connections. And pressures.

Increasingly, those pressures may leap from the realm of entertainment and enter into social interactions and judgments. "Competitive consumption" is how Harvard economist Juliet Schor describes the current climate of acquisition in *The Overspent American*, asserting that across economic lines, social pressures to possess more—and more upscale items—are greater than ever. You may not be in the same economic league as the fictional characters in mass media, or have the massive wardrobe budgets that television shows do to create the same look or "lifestyle." But the objects the characters have may inform what you want—and what you think your friends should have. These days, she says, people believe the pursuit of "keeping up" materially with friends, colleagues and neighbors—the Joneses, Wein-bergs, Santiagos, or anyone else—isn't a matter of status, but sur-vival. According to Schor's research, spending is now perceived by most people as a "defensive" maneuver: If you want to stay in the social game, you'd better ante up with objects.

What's Happened?

The current climate of consumption does not necessarily prompt a Pavlovian response for a certain brand of potato chips, or make us rush, lemminglike, to buy a sport utility vehi-cle because the guy down the street has one. But whether one's annual family income is $25,000 or $250,000, whether one is seven or seventy, to live in such an environment is to be subject to the promise of possessions.

And even if we don't wholeheartedly embrace all those mes-sages touting the power of possessions, we're listening to them. Over the last three decades, per-capita consumption has risen 62 percent. In recent years, credit card debt has reached record highs, personal-saving rates have hit new lows, and more people declared personal bankruptcy than graduated from college. According to the U.S. Census Bureau, the size of an average new house has expanded one and a half times since 1970. At the same time, one of the fastest-growing businesses today is in providing storage space for people's excess stuff. We might not define a din of materialistic messages as "pressure tactics" or even influential in our own spending habits. But clearly, something out there is sinking in for somebody.

We feel the need to buy more. But what do we value most? According to a recent Roper Starch Worldwide study, Americans' highest priority is protecting family. Other top values include honesty, stable personal relationships, and self-esteem. Interestingly, "power" came in last as an important value.

Okay, we may not admit we're power-hungry, but spending in recent years would indicate we're seeking something powerful from possessions. How does faith in the power of ownership intrude on what we truly want? Several possible ways:

Getting, spending, and maintaining devours time and energy. "Dollar, dollar, dollar!" That's what a low-budget film director was rumored to have shouted when things got slow on the set. With the price of production measured in day rates and equipment rentals, every wasted second meant money lost. Hoping to hasten the process, he would hop about, hollering.

Time is money, goes the old adage. But is it? The big difference between time and money, unless you happen to be on a film set, is that you can earn more money once it's spent. But time is not a renewable resource: Once it passes, it's gone.

Every week, the average American spends six hours shopping—and plays with his or her children just forty minutes. And the time working couples spend talking to each other? About twelve minutes a day, according to the 1997 PBS documentary *Affluenza.*

Spending money on stuff and maintaining possessions takes time. And time that could be spent on something more valuable and lasting may get lost in the process.

The promise of possessions may jumble priorities.   Have it all—and have it *now*. A quick fix can be lots of fun. And it may even work sometimes. But belief in ownership to give fast answers may have repercussions. Faith in objects may nudge it-self ahead of all else, overwhelming other aspirations.

Not long ago, a student of mine missed a deadline for an important paper. Looking exhausted, she wrote an essay in class explaining why:

> I am so tired. School is my number one priority, and I am determined to get a college education so that I can go to law school one day. But I have to work all the time now, because I bought a new car which costs $500.00 a month. As a result, I have no time to study. After I've worked all day I'm even too tired to go out with friends.

C'mon, kiddo. What's really the number-one priority here? The student didn't note the pleasure the car gave her, only the problems of paying for it. What was she really getting out of having the new car? What was the effect on her life—and having what she really wanted?

Owning can get confused with doing.   In the modern world, "materializing" means investing objects with meaning. In the "If only I owned 'x', then I would do/feel 'y'" setup of materializing, buying something seems like a reasonable guarantee of overcoming obstacles—any obstacle. The act of purchasing something is so closely linked with achieving personal success that "buying" and "being" may get confused: Buy the rowing machine and you'll be in shape. Buy a particular perfume, and you'll be more appealing and content. Owning, then, may become one with the accomplishment or feeling.

Obviously, in reality, it's hard work to get in shape or get to the place where you feel content with yourself, and the mere purchase of an exercise machine or fragrance isn't going to magically make these things happen for anyone. But faith in the power of possessions can make anything seem possible—even easy—with the right purchase. And it may get in the way of actually acting.

Owning can be a reason for not *doing.*   In the movie *Jingle All the Way*, Arnold Schwarzenegger plays a father obsessed with getting his young son the hot superhero toy-of-the-moment for Christmas. He's let his kid down many times before—not showing up when he says he will, for example—but this time, by golly, he's going to keep his promise.

Predictably, after many harrowing adventures, he gets a hold of the action figure. The kicker, of course, is that the kid didn't really care that much about having the toy. What he wanted was his dad.

It's familiar, and it's quite a tearjerker. What parent wouldn't try to go to the ends of the earth to make their kid happy? And what parent, at least once, hasn't given a gift in an effort to make everything okay with their child, to right wrongs—say, not spending enough "quality time" together?

So maybe we're all guilty of the occasional purchasable solution to assuage mixed feelings about not doing something with—or for—our kids. In the short term, it seems like a viable solution. But what values does it communicate in the long run? And what, ultimately, does the material solution do to address the real problem?

Fast-forward a few years to another holiday movie, *I'll be Home for Christmas*. Here, Jake is a snotty California college kid who will only deign to spend the holidays with his family back East if Dad promises him a '57 Porsche. Sure, Jake's wild 'n' wacky cross-country trek jingles a few sentimental "true meaning of the holidays" bells along the way, but what's really driving him to get home is the hope of getting a cool old car. Not doing the right thing. Not trying to make his old Dad happy. Not even a grudging sense of obligation.

Again, it's only a movie. But the notion of relationships guided by material promises has an ugly element of truth. And as a vision of Christmas Future, it's not a pretty picture.

The pursuit of "satisfaction" may heighten wants.   Faith in material solutions has a funny way of renewing and reproducing itself. Once you sail into the mythical land of Customer Satisfaction, where products fulfill every desire, pretty soon you notice another ship setting sail for a place where there's the potential for even *more* satisfaction. The product you already own is okay, but think of how much *greater* the satisfaction could be with something else you can buy! It's hard to resist the urge to hop on.

"He who knows enough is enough will always have enough," wrote Lao-tzu some 2,500 years ago.

The environment that emphasizes acquiring "more" over contentment in "enough" fuels faith that there's always something more desirable out there. And in the current climate, the possibility that you could be even *better* sated with yet another purchase is ever-present.

It promotes feeling inadequate.   Well, duh, as some younger consumers might say. Let's face it: There are a million ways to feel bad about yourself. If you didn't know them already, well, there are plenty of prompts today to pinpoint each failing—and provide solutions through ownership.

But if possessing something can make everything better, then *not* having the material solution may put the problem in a grim spotlight. And possibly distort and enlarge it.

Laura, thirty-five, described a difficult period of time during her divorce when merely seeing what she didn't own impeded her usual ability to think reasonably—and prompted an over-whelming sense of inadequacy:

> One day I got lost in a very upscale neighborhood. Each house was beautifully maintained, with expensive cars parked out-side. The place looked like a picture out of a catalog, and it felt like I had entered Brigadoon, the storybook place where everyone is happy all the time. For a minute, the neighbor-hood became the land of intact families, loving relationships, and some kind of wonderful sense of order—everything I felt I was lacking at that time. Just seeing those things that I didn't have was enough to make me feel living there would solve everything. And knowing it wasn't possible made everything in my own life seem worse.
>
> I knew it was time for my marriage to end, no matter what. But what I did with the image of the cars, the houses, and well-dressed people took control of my own sense of reality. At that moment, all those things encapsulated my own feelings of per-sonal failure.

Quantification meets communication.   One of the earliest concepts humans learn is comparing: Before the development of reading, writing, or formal math skills, a child can tell us whether something is bigger or smaller, shorter or taller, greater or lesser. As children develop into adults, the comparisons become more complex, but the principle remains a way of understanding the world.

Of course, some things can't be quantified. You can't put a number on important, internal values such as truth, love, protecting and honoring your family, self-respect, or acceptance. You can, however, compare objects. And materializing sets up a framework where just about anything—human beings and values alongside inanimate objects—can be quantified.

Incessantly asked to weigh the features and benefits of products, we may be in danger of applying the same criteria to people and relationships. Does buying an expensive crib mean you love your baby more? Of course not. But the connection between the quality of your attachment to your child and the quantity of money you're willing to spend is clearly, constantly defined.

And the quest to quantify human qualities has never been pursued more enthusiastically. Intelligence, "emotional intelligence," and even personality traits are increasingly assessed and ranked, like the various features of, say, a new washing machine. Years ago, Bo Derek rated a "10" in the eponymous movie that made her famous for a flash. Since the character did little more than wander vaguely, swinging her beaded braids, it wasn't exactly a full portrait of a real woman, nor was it intended to be. But these days, the obvious objectification of *10* has gone one step further, hairsplitting into scrutiny of separate mind, spirit, and body parts, not unlike that of cuts of chicken. And for anything that doesn't make the grade, there's a product to improve it.

To some extent, this approach may help us feel we have control. But it doesn't take into account what can't be measured: the student with a low test score who shows a remarkable ability for writing, the introverted personality that blossoms because of a fortuitous experience. Unlike products, people are magnificently unpredictable and complex: The whole is more than the sum of parts.

However, applying the same criteria to people as products is reinforced now more than ever—and it doesn't do a lot to build on values that can't be quantified.

Objects as answers may get in the way of growth.   Faith in possessions links ownership with overcoming the impossible: No loss is so great, no pain so harsh, or no relationship so difficult that it can't be turned around by a purchase. No talent is so elusive, no quality so rare that it can't be acquired in the form of a material object: Anything is possible with the right tools.

Optimistic? Of course. Realistic? Gimme a break.

Experience—feeling and acting on everything from pain and suffering to joy and pleasure—makes people grow. However, the connection between real growth and experience gets short shrift in the framework of materialism. Hey, when experience is synonymous with ownership, why bother to *actually* experience anything?

The "virtual" nature of materialized solutions—so easy, so immediate—may intrude on the process of actually growing. Hope springs eternal: It's easy to feel that building the new house will, somehow, suddenly make family gatherings for the holidays less emotionally difficult. It's easy to buy into the idea that owning the more expensive piano will be the catalyst to make your child want to practice. And given the current climate, it's even easy to believe that ownership of objects that may inspire admiration or envy from other people might be the key to inspiring genuine self-love.

But while it's easy to believe in the myriad, near-magical properties of ownership, what good does that really do? As I started to question my own expectations of material objects, it led me to consider an alternative: that transformation is an ongoing process that works from within, not a product that one, perhaps, could do without.

A retired physician who runs an arboretum once told me that trees grow in spirals. The concentric circles you see in a stump mark years of growth, swirling through time from the inside out. This process of growth occurs gradually, with events in the tree's life—a tough winter, a dry summer—appearing with differing rings. In the slice of the tree, we can see the summation of centuries of life. What we can't see is the daily process, the spiraling moments of experience that slowly add up to circles.

The doctor in the arboretum mused on whether humans grow in spirals as well. While you can't take a cross section of a person, the same idea might apply. The circles don't accumulate from the outside in; growing doesn't mean adding something externally. The spirals that add up to a lifetime in a tree are much like experiences that add up to a life in a person, the incremental culmination of working and living through both good times and bad.

We're vulnerable to believing in the shortcut of "adding on" through material solutions. You don't have to be a doctor—or a tree expert—to understand that the "outside-in" approach to growth probably doesn't work for people any more than it does for trees. And it may derail the actual experience that real growth requires.

In both old fairy tales and modern life, materializing gains momentum from the promise of power. Sure, possessions can be powerful. But how much do they really deliver on what we want most?

As I became immersed in researching materialism and its power, I tried applying some logic to find an answer: If materializing creates something tangible out of a hope, dream, or desire, but it doesn't give you want you really want, then "dematerializing" could mean retrieving that spirit from objects, recognizing them for what they are—objects. A process of dematerializing might work to break faith in the answer of ownership, taming expectations of possessions.

For me, and for the scores of people I interviewed—a group united by nothing except that they were all consumers—that couldn't mean renouncing worldly goods for a more "simple" life, since human needs and desires are complex, no matter where or how you happen to live. And while it seemed like a great idea, in theory, to just say no to popular culture prompts—or those of my kids' peers, for example—chances are, it's a lot more successfully said than done. Besides, I wasn't sure it could do anything to address the real issue at hand: individual wants and needs.

Considering these alternatives, I came to believe that challenging the power of possessions has to be a personal process with no "right" answers except those that help us to have what we really want. Dematerializing began to mean exploring our own, often complicated relationships with material objects, considering what possessions can and cannot do for our own lives, and exploring where belief in the magic of the material may intrude on belief in ourselves and other people. And perhaps most of all, it meant thinking about what's enough—and what isn't.

We live in a material world, perhaps more focused on the powers of material objects than ever before. And that's life. But while it's impossible to control the ever-present answer of ownership, it's possible to question it, and how it may affect what we want most.

When I first began exploring my own relationship with materialism, I wanted quick solutions. I wanted fast answers. Instead, what I got were stories from people—stories of the power of love, hope, and personal courage as well as of despair, of frustration, and of yearning for "something else." Stories of being overwhelmed, but also stories of gifts that had no price and contentment that couldn't be quantified. And over time, what I realized was this: Having what you want and wanting what you have isn't so much about finding an answer, but asking the questions.

What power do we seek from objects, and why? Most important, how can we work to retrieve that power from possessions—to have what we most value?

2

AT PEACE WITH THE PAST

"It's hard to say, but I do want it, and I want it terribly!"
He spoke with unusual candor and feeling. This seemed
more than his well-known possessiveness. "I'm not sure
why. . . If I had one solid piece of furniture, one object I
could point to, that would remind me of how happy
we all were, of how we used to live. . . "

—JOHN CHEEVER, "THE LOWBOY"

At first, just one or two items disappeared during a visit: a chipped candy dish here, an old mixing bowl there. They were things of little value, items that might turn up on a table at a yard sale. But after she left, something was always missing.

The brothers and sisters started to notice, and so did their aging mother, living alone in the house where her children had grown up. With each holiday visit, it became more apparent that Catherine was walking off with things from the house.

Why would she do that? Of all the children in the family, Catherine was the most successful professionally. She earned a lot of money and the respect of her colleagues, lived in a sprawling house with a pool, and drove a new, expensive car. She took luxurious vacations and gave extravagant presents. She could easily afford to buy her own mixing bowls and candy dishes, ones far nicer than those disappearing from her modest childhood home. And while Catherine was always a little difficult when dealing with her mother and siblings, she wasn't a thief. As far as anyone in the family knew, she'd never stolen a thing in her life.

When her mother decided to sell the house and move into a condominium, things turned even stranger. Catherine was against the move, adamant that her mother hold onto the family house. But her mother was equally stubborn; the old house and yard were too much for her, and she wanted a change. She couldn't cart thirty years' accumulation of possessions to an apartment, and told her four grown children they could take what they wished. The rest she'd sell.

Then Catherine began laying claim—as her cousin who told me this story put it—"to anything she could get her hands on." No more spiriting away the odd ashtray in her purse and thinking nobody would notice. While her siblings watched in disbelief, Catherine started making more frequent, solitary trips to visit her mother—for the sole purpose, it seemed, of taking what she thought was hers. Catherine would fly into town for a day to take away a suitcase filled to bursting with photographs, valuable old books, silver, and other things from her childhood house, never asking anyone else if they might like them.

Odder still, she also hauled home the ancient, enormous ice-cream maker that had been broken for years, the age-stained pillows when she'd just redecorated her own living room, and the ugly eggcups that wouldn't fetch more than a few quarters at a tag sale. Nobody else in the family wanted these things. But why did Catherine need to take *everything*?

This pattern took its toll. Thanksgiving dissolved into a disagreement over the sideboard that had always been in the dining room. Accusations of greed and ganging up flew across the table. Ancient arguments arose, opening old wounds. Dinner ended in tears.

Catherine's story is familiar: The players change and the monetary value of the items involved varies, but sentiment stays the same. Who knows what went on years before that prompted Catherine to seek something in the objects from the house? Who knows what that something was—and still is?

Catherine could simply be dismissed as strange, but her actions are intriguing, especially if you don't happen to be in her family. While most of us don't sit around endlessly blaming or praising Mom, Dad, and siblings or old teachers, bosses, friends, or enemies for our inner child's emotional state, past experiences are part of who we are now. And the meaning that objects acquire over the years may live on.

The question here isn't whether past experiences among siblings, parents, or friends play out with possessions—because clearly, they can—but why? How do happy or hurtful times from the past affect our current relationship with objects—and people? Most important, how can we extract old power associated with possessions to feel at peace with the past—and enhance how we live in the present?

Past Imperfect

In an advertisement on British television, people go back in time and give advice to their younger selves. Imagine being able to tell yourself to take better care of your teeth, buy the stock before it skyrockets, or steer clear of that person with whom you had that long-term, destructive relationship!

Alas, as Aristotle once wrote, "God himself lacks this power alone/To make what has been done undone." Of course you can't change your past self, no matter how appealing the prospect. Still, the desire to come to terms with an imperfect past is strong. And if you can't really go back and alter the course of your own history, you can try to make up for it in the present.

Which is where the power of possessions may move in. Connections to certain objects may remain, like a photographic image on the heart. And what you once had and lost—or wanted and never had—can take root in the mind in the form of owning something now. Fixing something that festered for decades may seem as close as your checkbook—or your childhood home.

How does the desire to feel at peace with the past and the ready answer of objects come together?

Revisiting "Rosebud".   In the famous opening scene of the 1941 film *Citizen Kane*, fictional tycoon Charles Foster Kane lies alone on his deathbed. His crabbed hand holds an old snow globe, a miniature winter scene encased in glass. The hand wavers, and the globe falls to the floor as he croaks out his single, dying word: "Rosebud."

Who or what was Rosebud, anyway? It's the question everyone asks throughout the movie, which chronicles the magnate's rise and fall. As we trace Kane's ascent to prominence and power by following the reporters who try to solve the riddle of Rosebud throughout the film, we learn he left home at a young age because of sudden, unexpected wealth. Kane's transformation from an idle, rich young man to idealistic journalist to would-be politician and patron unfolds, and we watch his desires—material and others—increase. When he dies, failed and alone in his huge estate, Xanadu, his collection of still-crated statues and other objects seems to stretch on for acres. And still he's asking for Rosebud.

"Maybe Rosebud was something he lost," opines one of Kane's business associates. Bingo! The reporters never discover the meaning of Rosebud, finally categorizing it as "a piece in a jigsaw puzzle—a missing piece." But we do. By the end we know Rosebud is the name of the sled Kane had as a boy before he left home, before he experienced wealth or power or failed relationships.

It's an "aha!" moment for many reasons. Okay, so Kane's early life with an alcoholic father and austere mother wasn't ideal. But the superwealthy adult Kane could have bought a hundred sleds—or a hundred thousand—just like the one rusting in that warehouse somewhere, for heaven's sake. No matter. It was only the Rosebud sled he lost, linked to another time, that counted. That was the only one he wanted to possess again.

Most of us don't live like the fictional Kane, and won't die as he did either. But it's safe to say that loss touches every life. Our lost Rosebuds may remain in our brains, the meaning they once held seemingly duplicable as material objects.

But can we really recover those "Rosebuds"? In the age of eBay, it might be easy to track down an old toy, but it's still tough to retrieve emotion: Had Charles Foster Kane made a miraculous recovery and found Rosebud again, what could it have actually done for him? Chances are he'd stow it with his other possessions once again. And move on to his next conquest.

Remaking the past.   If striving for what we once had and lost is seductive, trying to get what we *didn't* have may be even more so. We hear a lot about making up for lost time, from missed opportunities to mistakes we once made. It's easy to believe that acquiring an object now will make up for something that disappeared long ago—or was never there.

Mary, a successful working mother of four, saw how she may still try to right the past with possessions:

> My older brother was academic, and the family's hope for the future. My sister was the homecoming queen, and the twins, who were younger than me, were great athletes. I was considered the dreamer who wouldn't amount to anything. And that position got played out when it came to getting clothing, gifts, you name it. At least it felt like it did.
>
> There's no question that I go overboard with buying my own children things now. And getting things for myself. I know that part of it is almost like revenge, to prove to everyone in my family that I've made it, despite what they thought. But the other side is that I still need to prove it to myself. I'm still trying to make everything all right with stuff, and that bothers me.

So what's wrong with getting things you once wanted but couldn't have in the past? Nothing. To have your own room when you always shared one, to buy a nice car because you can, to give your kids things you could only dream about having at their age—of course it's satisfying, maybe even empowering.

But how far can purchasing-power go in fixing what was once, well, wrong?

In *The Great Gatsby*, Jay Gatsby was once rejected by the beautiful Daisy Buchanan, because he didn't rate socially or financially in her upper-crust world. Years later, Gatsby is fabulously wealthy and still pines for the now-married, elusive Daisy. In the hope of winning her, he buys the mansion directly across the bay from her house, conspires with the novel's narrator, Nick, to meet her again, and invites her to his house.

It's a famous scene in the novel: Gatsby shows Daisy his grand house and possessions, and overcome by the moment he's dreamed of for years, he even shows off his shirts, "piled like bricks in stacks a dozen high." Nick tells how Gatsby "began throwing them one by one before us, shirts of sheer linen and thick silk and fine flannel which lost their folds as they fell and covered the table in many-colored disarray. While we admired he brought more and the soft rich heap mounted higher—shirts with stripes and scrolls and plaids in coral and apple green and lavender and faint orange with monograms of Indian blue. Suddenly, with a strained sound Daisy bent her head into the shirts and began to cry stormily."

Why is Daisy crying? It's a good guess that the beauty of the shirts doesn't really move her to tears, but what does? Her own messed-up youth, missed opportunities, and current marriage to another man who's a rich, immoral, biased buffoon? Sorrow for a man trying, with near-desperation, to right her own past mistakes? Sadness at his attempt to alter time with a parade of stuff, no matter how late?

While F. Scott Fitzgerald's 1925 novel about the superrich is as much about social conventions of the time as it is about human nature, it still speaks volumes about attempts to recapture something from the past via objects. Breaking free from his poverty-stricken past, Gatsby has gotten his shirts, and then some. But he never really gets the girl.

❀　　❀　　❀

Most of us don't really believe that there's a rewind button in life, magically accessible by buying things. Rationally, we know it's a bit far-fetched to think deleting old hurts, disappointments, deprivation, or even indifference is a matter of acquiring objects now. Still, there's a reason that scene in *The Great Gatsby* still strikes a chord: The power of possessions may make us believe we can.

Like the one that got away in *Moby-Dick*, objects may take on whale-like proportions: In efforts to fill in gaps, retrieve something or right wrongs from the past, the pursuit of possessions may overwhelm actually addressing what's really missing.

The trouble with seeking feeling in objects is that while possessions come and go, the rotten feeling may remain. So here's a different way to look at past deficiencies: How did *not* having something in the past enrich you? How did it shape who you are now in positive ways?

And then there's the question of what you now seek. There's no dispute that settling an old score may be satisfying, but can an object—or many—actually do that? The "never" in "never enough" can stretch on for eternity, whether you're talking about objects or behavior. And for most of us, there isn't a magical moment when someone who tormented us says, "Eureka! I've treated you badly for years, and now I'm going to mend my ways!"

Since you can't count on that flash of insight from the outside coming anytime soon, coming to terms with what you didn't have may be a matter of turning inward. For a moment, forget the perpetrators of past crimes against your spirit and ask yourself a simple question. What do you really want to possess at *this* point in time?

Past Perfect

Despite recent, record prosperity, more than 50 percent of adults of all ages in this country believe that things were better in the past than they are today. That's a change in attitude from the mid-1970s, when more people surveyed preferred the present, according to *American Demographics* magazine. Even if you do not have an idealized view of the old days, someone out there does. So why does the past now look so great?

The word "nostalgia" comes from a couple of ancient Greek words meaning "return home" and "pain"; "homesickness," in other words. With nostalgia, the feasibility of *really* returning home—through a cavalcade of Broadway revivals or déjà vu fashion, for example—hardly matters. What's important is the enticing *idea* of home in the past, never attainable, but always somehow preferable to the present.

Let's face it: Nostalgia is a gold mine on many levels. Romancing the past is a winning prospect, since hard-edged reality has a hard time competing with warm-and-fuzzy reenactments. And it's spawned countless "olde-fashioned" products, "vintage" reproductions, and movies and television shows. Sure, maybe bygone times didn't make every clan into those close and caring Waltons, but we can imagine it did. Maybe being young in the '50s, '60s, or '70s—a time before, say, XXX-rated dot coms or cloning—wasn't always an innocent laugh fest, but crafted into fiction and images, it can look pretty good compared to now, particularly if you didn't happen to be around for the real thing. Nostalgia is handy because it sets an emotional standard that can't be fact-checked.

And just as that antique-reproduction lamp sells because it evokes another time, looks cool today, and doesn't have the nasty frayed cord or require hard-to-find light bulbs like the authentic old one, personal nostalgia can lead to reinvention. But unlike that lamp, reinvention through personal nostalgia may distort. Polished up and edited, memories become stories, stories become myths.

Since myths exaggerate by nature, it's hard to live up to them. Myths involving tangible objects in the here and now—as opposed to old stories of action, which can always be questioned—are especially hard. Sure, an object can always be reproduced, but it's hard to reproduce the feeling you may have associated with the original object, and in its time and place. Still, bolstered by a culture that exults in the tangible as a means of expressing the deepest feelings, viewing the past through rose-colored glasses gets personal. Objects linked with long-ago warm feelings may move into center stage as a kind of insurance against disappointment in the present. Or future.

The promise of possessing Past Perfect has developed over the years in a number of ways:

Competition with "firsts".   It's no coincidence that we're inundated with messages that begin by setting the stage with misty memory: "Remember the first time you. . . ." The product, of course, promises an experience that moves beyond special and into the singular: a "first," again and again. Photographs and other images aid the illusion: no matter how contrived, a tiny detail in a happy Thanksgiving scene may tap into a long-forgotten moment. The picture of the lovely young woman walking on the beach can set off a reverie of memory. The thrilled child with his new bicycle sets the stage for suspension of disbelief. The message? The past is within your grasp.

The problem is that when the sequel is a rehash, it's rarely as good as the original, at least when the original has been teased into shape by tricks of time. And within the promise of reexperiencing an emotional high point is the threat of grim finality: Your peak was in the past, so you'd better turn back and try to recapture it now.

Holidays and collective consumerism.   "Better in the past" may or may not have a basis in the material, but through images, a kind of collective memory exists. The translation of traditional celebrations into the traditions of consuming have accelerated in the last half-century, and, even if you don't have halcyon memories of a holiday, pictures of an idealized past version are everywhere. The caption? With the right purchases, this is the year you'll finally have all that warmth, good feeling, and fun of yesteryear yourself.

Take Christmas. In the mid-nineteenth century, when Englishman Charles Dickens wrote about Scrooge's transformation from miserly old humbugger into merry old soul he created a vision of familial warmth and gratitude surrounding the holiday (remember Tiny Tim's touching delight in getting Christmas *dinner*, never mind receiving toys?) that crossed the Atlantic and settled in for the long haul here. Images and messages of an "old-fashioned" Christmas took root; by 1920, when "Xmas" advertising first multiplied in earnest, nostalgia for those simple old days began to emerge. Alongside hundreds of newspaper ads for de rigueur gifts, one for None Such mincemeat promised to produce "Christmas mince pies. . . 'like Mother used to make.'"

Backlit by the ever-present glow of media imagery, holidays now seem to issue a challenge: Can you make this The Best Christmas Ever? Sure, the view of the tree changes when you grow from three feet to six, and the miracle of presents on Christmas morning may never match a child's-eye view. But that doesn't mean that you can't try: To avoid disappointment, deck the halls more, get a bigger tree, and buy twice as many presents this year!

Glancing into the rearview mirror of expectation doesn't stop with Christmas or other holidays. Childhood excitement of getting ready for old-time summer fun or going back to school have emerged as full-blown shopping seasons. A whiff of newly sharpened number-two pencils isn't necessarily the modern-day equivalent of Marcel Proust's taste of a madeleine cake (which brought back remembrances of things past) for everyone, it may touch upon old feeling—and the possibility of besting the experience this time around, as long as you buy right.

Inner children revisited.   Think of baseball cards, the currency of ten-year-olds. Talk to grown men and they may start rhapsodizing about the happy hours they spent poring over those pictures of heroes, the time devoted to memorizing their idols' stats, and the drama of making trades. Keep asking and you might hear about the miraculous day they found, along with the nearly unchewable stick of bubble gum, the rare rookie card they'd always wanted. Dig a little deeper and you might hear how the cardboard cards constituted a world apart from parents and school, preceding the time when you worried about whether a girl thought you were a geek.

The rest of the story is often the same: The boy grew older, and the beloved cards were moved aside to make way for other interests. Stored in a shoe box at the back of the closet, they were nearly forgotten. Until the day, many years later, that the boy who is now a man goes to look for his old cards. But they're gone, lost in a move or tossed out by Mom years ago.

Times change: The cards have become currency once again, collectibles at a steeper price. The current, astronomical cost of that rookie card you once treasured becomes the stuff of news stories; what once existed only in the world of boys now enters the world of business. Forget your dog-eared collection: Crisp corners become crucial.

The business of collecting now is a far cry from the assortment of cheap cards that made for some happy childhood moments. The value of regaining that priceless childhood sentiment, though, may get deeper with years. "The bigger the boys, the bigger the toys," goes the old saying. In this case, though, the toy stays the same; the desire for that intangible "something" that the cards once provided may be what grows.

That's not to say that every baseball-card collector is desperately trying to relive his youth through a pile of cardboard. But the surge of interest in old sports cards, dolls, lunch boxes, and the like, along with the widespread passion among adults for new beanbag animals, plastic figures, and other items once limited in appeal to children demonstrates adults' desire to bring some piece of Past Perfect into their present with objects. The high-flying prices of these "kidult" items also show that the perceived value of finding that elusive "something" is greater than ever.

✿   ✿   ✿

You can't bottle the sensation of cheerfully playing jacks in the sunshine on a summer day, but you can own the old jacks that remind you of that time; you may not be able to recapture the exact feeling of being safe and snug as a child, but you can eat the same comforting canned soup at home as you did twenty years ago. The yearning to recapture what you once had and lost due to the simple passing of time, or something more traumatic, is perfectly reasonable. Except that it may be a never-ending quest, one that may intrude on actually having what we *can* have now.

Even if you now own a baseball-card collection that would have been the envy of your old neighborhood, everyone knows you can't go home again. The game changes, even if the objects are the same. But given the number of messages we receive on reclaiming a feeling, an experience, or an idealized situation that never really existed, it's easy to believe we can try.

Several years ago, I read about a man who built a full-size, professional-quality baseball field in his backyard. It was for his young son, he said. He could build it—so he did. The story reminded me of the movie *Field of Dreams,* where a man is struck by a seemingly irrational urge—complete with a voice others can't hear—to build a baseball diamond on his farmland. "If you build it," says the voice, "they will come." Though nearly everyone thinks he's lost his mind, the man builds the field, eventually playing host to the ghosts of baseball greats. The defining moment of the movie comes when the man's long-dead, baseball-playing father—still youthful after all the years—shows up for a game of catch with his son.

In the end, living people come to the field, too, and dreams become reality. It's a beautiful idea: The man, following his heart, isn't really crazy. Possessed by something stronger than reason, he builds what he wants. And in the end, he gets what he needs: He tosses a ball again with his long-gone dad.

It's different in real life, of course: Most of us can't build a field for "them" to come. Then again, we don't have to. It's possible to go about finding our own fields of dreams—and make peace with the past—by acknowledging what, realistically, we are able to have in the present. Rather than turning our energy to reproducing a glorious memory, recapturing something long-gone, or righting old wrongs through possessions, we can consider what we have gained from the past. And find the singularity, the "firsts," of experiences now.

The Monkey on Our Backs

Old associations with objects may be the stuff of happy dreams, but they can also become a living nightmare. I once visited a summer house that had a line running down the middle. This line had been painted years ago, when an argument between two brothers over ownership of the house erupted for the last time. Even though they both continued to come to the house in the summer, the brothers no longer spoke to each other, and neither crossed the line defining their separate spaces.

It was awkward, to say the least. Although my host—one of the brothers—didn't seem especially bothered by it, there was something awful about being a guest in a house where you felt, well, invisible to half of its occupants. And it was confusing. Were you crossing into enemy territory by using the wrong bathroom? Would using the unmarked milk in the refrigerator constitute theft? I was afraid to ask. The feud between the Hatfields and McCoys, part of American legend for their generations-long vicious battles over property boundaries, has finally fizzled. But their spirit quietly lived on within this family.

Who hasn't heard of fights waged over ownership of things large and small? Some may sound stupid, but certainly some are justified. Still, the looming power of possessions has a way of making people unable to see the forest for the trees, especially when the "tree" is something both want. Sure, it can end amicably. But it can also result in severed ties and a ludicrous line down the middle of a house that turns a once-pleasant place into tension-filled territory.

Which comes first: the object of desire in question or the problematic relationship surrounding it? I once heard about a pair of octogenarian sisters who, after a few glasses of sherry, spent every family gathering arguing over the ownership of a pet monkey they had as children. Never mind that the monkey had been dead for a good seventy years.

Clearly, you can beat a dead horse—or monkey, as the case may be—for eternity. But who was really doing the beating here? Years later, the memory of the pet, and whatever it meant to the two sisters, seemed to be in control of how they behaved with one another. The monkey, so to speak, was still on their backs.

As anyone who has ever been involved in an argument over an object knows, knocking that monkey from its lofty and powerful perch isn't easy. It may not even be possible. But then, what does it give to anyone now? Is the price of a long-dead monkey or your great-grandmother's ring or a house or anything else in the middle of a conflict worth the price it may exact on the rest of life?

It may be. Then again, it may not. Annual family get-togethers could be more pleasant for these two sisters—not to mention for the rest of their family—if they finally laid the idea of the monkey to rest. Finally gaining possession of your great-grandmother's ring may be a victory, and you may think of her every time you wear it, but at what expense to the relationship with your cousin who wanted it, too?

The Old Testament tells the story of King Solomon, who is called upon to settle a dispute between two women. Each had a baby; one baby died and the other lived. Now each claims to be the living baby's mother; neither mother is willing to back down. Finally, King Solomon calls for a sword and says, "Divide the living child in two, and give half to the one, and half to the other."

One of the women pleads for the child to be given away, and not slain; the other says, "Let it be neither mine nor thine, but divide it." Wise King Solomon gives the child to the woman who gives up her claim on the child so that it may live, knowing that her unselfish act can only demonstrate the love of the true mother.

Arguments over possessions aren't generally life and death situations, and they can include a compromise that isn't as drastic as cutting a baby, or anything else, in two. The point here is that resolving disputes over "ownership" involves choices. And those choices often mean deciding between preserving or maintaining a relationship or gaining possession of something.

You may be right, of course. But at what price? What do you lose, now and in the future, by waging—or even winning—a battle over an object?

In the Moment

When I was a college student, I once showed up for a philosophy class taught by a Very Important Professor. The teacher's reputation for being both brilliant and unorthodox was legendary on campus, and the first class meeting was standing room only. In the packed room, he told us that admission to his class would be determined by a written "audition," an essay answering this question: "What is 'being'?" On the basis of what we wrote in the next hour, we were told, he would select only a few students.

Talk about intimidating. At that point, several people walked out. The rest of us slowly got out paper and pencils. After fifteen minutes, nearly everyone around me was scribbling frantically. So far, I had written a grand total of two words: "Being is."

What would gain entrance into the coveted class? I'd always been a pretty good student, and could usually figure out what teachers wanted. But I'd never taken a philosophy class. I didn't have a clue about quoting the great thinkers or even the not-so-great ones. His question threw me for a loop.

Being? Most of my life, then and now, consisted of "showing up," to paraphrase Woody Allen. Showing up to class, to the library, to my job on campus, to dinner with my boyfriend, to some party or another. What was "being"? I didn't have a single profound thought.

The minutes ticked by. While my fellow students were starting on their second sheets of paper, I still had just two words. The lucky ones were starting to finish, triumphantly handing in their papers while I continued to stare at the page.

And still I had nothing. No sudden flash of inspiration. No startling, original insight. Zip. Staring balefully at my paper, I realized that time was nearly up, and that I was no closer to an answer than I had been an hour earlier. What was being? No way could I unlock that secret in the remaining few minutes of class. Still, I had to hand in something. So, throwing grammatical caution to the wind, I stuck a period on the end of what I'd written. It was lame, I knew, but at least I hadn't just given up. The last to leave, I turned in what was surely the shortest answer: "Being is."

Writing off the philosophy essay, and class, as a total loss, I scurried away and signed up for something else. But a week later, when I checked to see who the lucky few were, I was shocked to find out I'd somehow made it into the class. The professor was either a complete idiot, I thought, obviously mistaking my loss for words for something more meaningful, or I had just gotten lucky. What I'd written seemed more suitable for a bumper sticker than serious study. In any case, I forgot about it, immersed once more in the business of showing up.

Years later, I discovered that in that college classroom, I'd unwittingly stumbled upon an idea that had been around for millennia. For many thousands of years, Eastern thinkers have explored the idea that "being," well, just *is*. Zen Buddhism shuns the confines of logic, comparison and even words to get to the core of existence. Baba Ram Dass's bywords of "be here now" revived the idea more recently. Today, "live in the moment" has resurfaced, appearing everywhere from pop songs to advertisements.

Being is.

Living in the moment is a lovely idea. To be free from experiences of the past and unfettered by worries of the future and live by savoring what is right here, right now is a beautiful notion. No wonder it's been around for so long.

But as a clever and somewhat cynical friend once observed as we looked out over some farmland, cows live in the moment, as do chickens. And save for acting on some brief, fleeting memory of a long-buried bone, so do dogs, for the most part. Animals live in, and for, the moment: now eating grass, now going back to the barn, now chasing a long-gone rabbit. Humans naturally don't, my friend added.

Not that either of us knew anything about animal behavior, and maybe the inner workings of the creatures we were observing were far richer than he imagined. But it seemed my friend had a good point about people. Put the "human" in "human being" and like it or not, you get past and future tenses along with the present. "Being is" encompasses both the gift and curse of memories, and the dreams and fears of the future. It includes the "was" and "will be" of our lives.

Certainly, we live in an environment that capitalizes on the complexities of merging past with present. We may want to figure out what went wrong and make it right, whether it involves an old monkey or an old house. We may want to seek revenge, or hold onto or reproduce something we once cherished. And objects can become answers, whether we really believe what we see. Like it or not, we're surrounded by messages that merge past, present, and future, aligning "be here now" with "buy here now."

Because connections between objects and old emotions are so strong, possessions *can* sometimes help you feel at peace with the past. Your grandfather's watch may bring back memories every time you look at it. Small things in your own house may remind you of the ways you've chosen to live differently from—or similarly to—your parents. And making cookies with the molds your grandmother used may spark a sense of continuity and tradition.

So maybe noticing those connections are part of being here now. Not forever seeking what you've missed. Not fighting a battle with objects over old anguish. Not hanging onto an ideal or the "not" in "not enough" that can continue forever.

And maybe one way of forging peace with the past is to work on finding purpose in the now. Which means, perhaps, going beyond the confines of glossy paper and film stock—or the myths of memory—to snap a "sense picture" of a moment of joy, of peace, of pure happiness that exists outside of the props of possessions and in the heart. It means considering experience, growth, and wisdom that is cumulative, not acquired with stuff. In the present.

Then and Now

Fred Stern is an "environmental artist" who uses sunshine and huge sprinklers to create giant rainbows in public spaces all over the world. He views the colorful, temporary arcs of light and water that he makes as a "bridge between the real and the

imaginary." Because water drops and sunlight vary, no two rainbows are ever the same. And due to minute differences in
points of view, no two people ever see quite the same rainbow.
Just as perception of rainbows is in the eyes of the beholder, so
is "the bridge between the real and the imaginary" when it
comes to the past and how it may relate to objects now.

Ask ten people to recount the same event they all witnessed
a decade ago, and you may get ten somewhat different stories.
Broad outlines may remain the same, but details will vary, colored by who the witness was then—and who they are today.
Unlike experience, however, objects appear to be constant: The
oak desk looks just as it did a hundred years ago.

What is "real"? What is "imagined"? Discerning between the
actual object and the meaning that it once held—and may continue to hold—is where things get complicated. As a creator of
fleeting works of beauty to celebrate world peace and unity,
Stern advocates beginning each day with a conscious moment
of "break-past" to evaluate the hold the past may have on moving forward into the future.

Fair enough. However, objects firmly wedged into memory
may not be so easily dislodged. Working to gain perspective on
the ways that old ideas of objects impact our lives now may
help us find what's missing, what we never had, and what we
may want or need now.

Not long ago, I learned of a man who, as a very young child,
survived the Holocaust in hiding. His memories of the house
where he was born were hazy, dotted with tiny details: a teapot
here, a rug there. For years, he had no desire to revisit the
country where he was born, but he eventually decided to take
his family there. It was an important and meaningful trip for all

the family members, and on their way to the airport in a cab, something very odd happened: He saw the teapot he remembered from childhood in the window of an antiques shop.

Here's another wartime story: A Japanese student of mine told of how her grandfather traveled frequently for business. Before one particularly long trip, he promised to bring his daughter a red parasol. A bomb hit his boat and he never returned. My student told of how her mother would speak frequently of her father's goodness, and of the red parasol that must have gone down with his ship.

Years later, when the daughter was a grown woman with grandchildren, she went to sea, seeking the place where her father's boat sank years earlier. She brought white lilies in memory, and perhaps mourning, for her long-dead father. As she cast the white flowers into the ocean, she swears she saw a red umbrella rise up from the white foam.

Miraculous? Perhaps. Did the woman really see a red umbrella, sunk for decades? Was the teapot really the same one the man remembered from his family's long-gone house? Does it matter? What's interesting is that each of these people, turning to parts of their past, found what they needed to find for peace in the present. Actually owning the long-gone object itself was not as important as finally possessing the idea of the object, not as something forever lost, but something found in the present.

To serendipitously find what was thought to be long-lost is a gift, perhaps, of fate. However, to become ready to discover it can be deliberate.

Taking the journey to find meaning from the past isn't always about revisiting old haunts. But it may mean taking action, a clearing out of past-attached clutter that may get in the way of having what we need now.

And it may involve a current reality check. What's real now—or imagined?

You can't do much about reproducing or righting holidays, but you can work on creating a feeling of warmth and security by spending time doing something with your spouse, children, or friends—other than endless shopping or decorating—now. You can't beg, borrow, or steal the past—or make another person be reasonable about ownership of objects—but you can mindfully withdraw your own emotional investment from the conflict.

You can ask how much objects and old meanings deliver what you want in the present. And while you can't make up for something you never got, you can think about this: Do you still need it?

3

~:~

GOOD IN YOUR SKIN

His motor car was poetry, tragedy, love and heroism.

—SINCLAIR LEWIS, *BABBITT*

It's a good-hair day. Basically, it's a good *everything* day, because she looks fabulous. Smiling, she shares her secret: She uses the pricier hair color, she purrs, "because I'm worth it." The actress's confidence is incredible, at least in a thirty-second advertising spot. Who *wouldn't* want to feel as worthy as she?

That self-assured woman was a fixture throughout my youth, the promise of things to come. She took many different forms, sold different stuff, but her message didn't alter: You *could* acquire deep-down confidence and contentment. Easily. Like a rallying cry of liberation, of emancipation from nameless oppressors, her tone shouted, "I am somebody. I am deserving. And aren't you, too?"

Even if it didn't register at a tender age, I later learned that it took dozens of people several hundred hours to produce this commercial message. I discovered there were aids such as hair and make-up artists, lighting experts, professional wardrobe people, and artful airbrushers in postproduction, not to mention the possible time over years the actress put in at the gym or a plastic surgeon's office. At some point I realized—a moment of modern-day innocence lost—that the actress didn't just bound out of bed one morning looking and feeling radiant, saying, "Think I'll tell the public the secret of my super self-esteem today—I hope there's a camera around!"

But even when I stopped swallowing this stuff hook, line, and sinker, the message, imprinted from childhood, continued to resonate for me. And for many other people as well, apparently. Clearly, self-esteem matters to Americans, regardless of how they've done financially; surveys show the vast majority of people earning $100,000 or more believe self-esteem is very important to success. The choice of hair color or whatever else Mr. or Ms. Self-Esteem of the moment happens to sell certainly capitalizes on a sense of smugness, but it also strikes at a deep desire: to feel valid and validated. To feel that one's own worth transcends petty concerns over, say, how much money you have to spend to achieve it. To feel good in one's own skin at any price.

While the Great Hair model declares emancipation through a hair product, though, you have to ask: Just who or what is this woman freeing herself *from*?

More than 200 years ago, when Thomas Jefferson wrote about rights to "life, liberty and the pursuit of happiness," he didn't specify that self-esteem was part of the picture. Still, it's hard to find real happiness when you feel awful about yourself. The idea that people should not only live freely but have the right to pursue what makes them happy—as opposed to putting up with the status quo or living unhappily with no power to change things for yourself—was a radical concept of citizenship. And self-worth is part of the notion that anyone, rich or poor, powerful or not, has the right to pursue and aspire to happiness.

This democratic ideal of an equal shot at happiness for all held innumerable, wondrous possibilities, and still does. No longer was happiness something simply desirable, left in the hands of one's Maker or leaders. It wasn't just a promise for the afterlife, after repeatedly suffering for survival in this life. Actively going for happiness—here, now—became a right. Sure, you're not *guaranteed* the right to feel good about yourself or anything else in your life, but under the law you're entitled to go for it.

The carpe diem aspect of the American tradition linking personal empowerment with political rights was, and still is, a remarkable concept. Of course, the *pursuit* of happiness is different from actually nailing the feeling down, but it's an important start.

Still, when you eliminate the idea that self-worth and happiness are part (or not) of destiny, do these qualities become, well, a destination? That destination, happiness somewhere on the horizon, has always included material goods, and with good reason. But how far do they go in delivering authentic self-esteem?

Of course, the answer depends on objects and expectations. Whether objects actually deliver self-worth and other aspects of happiness is up to individuals. However, in a materialized environment, the dominant external message is that they do—always.

The promise of self-worth is as near as the next purchase, that destination of happiness is frequently presented *as* the object: "Let the neighbors know you've arrived ahead of schedule," says the car ad. To have "arrived" is the goal; happiness, self-esteem, feeling good in your skin, is as close as the new car in the driveway. At least, for a while. The problem is that the "destination" keeps changing with new products. And there's always a new rung to reach on the ladder of self-worth.

Can money bring happiness? Well, of course it does, particularly if it's what comes between you and, say, not eating. And even if you're not talking about bare-bones survival, it's safe to say that having money can help people be happy. But does *more* money bring more happiness? Not necessarily. As social psychologist David G. Myers has observed, studies repeatedly show the correlation between increased income and happiness is weak. As he puts it, "Once comfortable, more money provides diminishing returns. The second piece of pie, or the second $100,000, never tastes as good as the first."

While the ability to buy objects can't balance every mood swing, there's no question that it is certainly part of happiness and may contribute to self-esteem in some way. But how much? And how does that link get forged?

In the 1970s, psychoanalyst Heinz Kohut came up with the term "self-object" to describe emotional attachments essential for normal growth and development. An infant's first self-object is his or her mother, the person who meets the baby's needs. Interactions with this person influence, among other things, future self-esteem and coping skills. Writing about disorders of the self, Kohut, with Ernest S. Wolf, identified two types of self-objects: "[T]hose who respond to and confirm the child's innate sense of vigour, greatness and perfection; and those to whom the child can look up and with whom he can merge as an image of calmness, infallibility and omnipotence." Put another way, the first self-object is cheerleader and god, in one fell swoop.

According to Kohut, as an infant grows, he becomes more independent, "internalizing" the care provided by the self-object to meet needs on his own. The quality of the child's attachment to the self-object, as well as his ability to "internalize" that care into his own sense of self, is key to healthy psychological development, goes the theory.

This process of internalization may involve a "transitional object"—say, a toy bear—that provides comfort to the child. Think of Linus's attachment to his beloved blanket, for example. While the longevity of the Peanuts character's need for his blanket no doubt surpassed any other in history (the comic strip ran for fifty years, after all), the human need for self-objects remains throughout life. Of course, outside the realm of comics, people grow up and change—and so do their self-objects.

As adults, most of us aren't dragging around a worn piece of flannel to help us feel more at ease in the world. But is it possible that we continue to seek "transitional" self-objects—external "regulators" of ourselves that we may call upon in vulnerable times—not just in other people or a higher power, but in actual objects?

Many personality problems can occur when early self-objects fail to provide what a developing self needs, says Kohut. Inadequate relationships with either the god or cheerleader in a young life—and the inability to incorporate these roles into one's own sense of self later—can result in what he called "fragmentation" of the self. A piece is missing; the personality is not quite whole. This fragmentation can result in major "issues," ranging from narcissism to seeing oneself as a pathetic bore.

Still, you don't need to have a serious personality disorder to feel a little insecure sometimes. You don't need to be suffering from separation issues with a baby blanket and your thumb to feel hungry for something more. If you put your mind to it, you can find a way to feel inadequate, with no help at all. And given the hundreds of messages we receive every day that not only pinpoint emotional needs or failures—those fragments of self, soul, mind, and body that may need some structural attention—but offer esteem-pledging solutions, it's no wonder we may buy into an emotional fix, no matter how flimsy, in the form of an object.

The pledge of products to provide a missing piece of self demands, of course, a willing participant. You must discard disbelief and embrace the idea that buying an object *can* somehow deliver the good feeling of a psychological cheerleader or all-powerful spirit. Of course, it's easier with some objects than with others; the hopes and dreams tied up in hair dye and cosmetics are a natural fit with the promise of "feeling good about yourself," since these products can and do provide some kind of change, albeit external. The leap of faith between object and self-object may be greater with other kinds of stuff, but then, belief is a powerful thing. Nearly any object can take on the qualities of an emotional elixir the moment before you own it.

As one woman said, "My own feel-good therapy is buying shoes. They always fit, even when I've gained ten pounds. I have way too many shoes, and I don't even like most of them, but it doesn't stop me from wanting another pair when I'm feeling bad about those pounds or something else. Even when I bought them I knew they weren't going to do what I wanted them to do for me."

As the aphorism goes, "When the going gets tough, the tough go shopping." But more likely, it's the vulnerable, seeking that external emotional regulator, who are most likely to buy into that belief. And who doesn't feel vulnerable at times? On the days when nothing is going right, buying stuff may offer the prospect of salvation. The solution to feeling less overwhelmed or getting your mind out of the dumps seems so accessible.

One self-described "shopper" in her thirties said, "It's easy to lose all your good sense when you're feeling bad. You see an answer, and go for it without thinking."

And, as she points out, sometimes the process of buying something works to improve your mood. You do feel better, or at least not as low, and manage to get through self-doubt for a while. But usually, she added, buying something when you feel shaken "feels good going down, like eating a doughnut. It's a fix to feed yourself when you feel hungry for something. Before you buy, you can't name what you really crave, but then you get pleasure in knowing you've just bought something, so the craving goes away for a while. It usually doesn't last, though, because nothing really changes. The satisfaction I get lasts about as long as eating that doughnut. I sometimes look at things I've bought when I was depressed, and get mad at myself. If I knew what was missing, I probably wouldn't do it."

It's doubtful that anyone actually views a new electronic gadget as a balm for a saddened soul, or really feels, in the long run, that serenity and self-esteem can be had for the price, say, of a scented candle. Still, something clicks. The promise that an object can deliver an internal sense of strength and well-being is obviously appealing. But why is the link between feeling good and buying something so effective in propelling desire, again and again, even when it may not work for long? And how can it distract from actually feeling good in your skin? And what about the question of alternatives: When the magic does-n't happen, how can we challenge belief in objects to deliver self-esteem—and find optimism elsewhere?

What's Different Now?

Have people always pondered personal happiness as much as they do today? A few thousand years ago, Aristotle explored happiness and self-esteem in its various aspects. He came to the conclusion that happy people are simply and basically happy, whatever their circumstances. Still the connection be-tween emotional well-being and objects may be there, and has grown stronger than ever in the last century. Here are some thoughts on *why:*

The birth of behaviorism in the marketplace.   In the early 1920s, noted American psychologist John B. Watson—known as the "founder of behaviorism"—first proposed the idea that the desire to feel good could translate into purchasing something, which led to principles about buying behavior still used today.

Intrigued by how rats learn things, Watson found that if you put food at the end of a "rat run," they'd scamper down to get

it. Learning that food might be at the end of the run, they'd re-
peat the behavior. But if you put a pane of glass in the middle
of the rat run and the rat smashed into it, the poor creature
would learn from that experience as well. And even when Watson removed the pane of glass, he found that the rat would no
longer dash to the food at the end of the run. In fact, the rat
might avoid going down the run altogether.

Today, all this conditioned-response behaviorist stuff sounds
pretty basic. But Watson had big ideas for his day: If rats' behavior could be influenced by the idea of reward or pain, why
not see if it worked with humans? In 1915, he discovered he
could use a rabbit to terrify an unfortunate child named Albert
by banging something loudly near the child's ear every time the
animal came close. He also reported that he could reverse this
response by introducing the animal to the child in a less unpleasant way. (Interestingly, by the late 1920s, Watson had produced a tome on child-rearing, which advocated that parents
avoid showing affection. The ideal child, he wrote, would be
"as free as possible from sensitivities to other people.")

Dismissed from his position as a professor of psychology of
Johns Hopkins University in 1920, Watson joined the "consumption engineers" of the day, bringing his "science of real
life" to work in advertising. Using the idea that happy feelings
could be the human equivalent of a rodent's piece of cheese,
Watson promoted the idea that the promise of an intangible reward for buying something would make people purchase it.
Again, this may not sound groundbreaking now, but it was rev-
olutionary at the time: Instead of just listing a product's attributes for consumers, the idea was to give 'em personal promise

and meaning. Rather than just extolling the high quality of the ingredients in baby powder, for example, Watson's product copy crows that "caring mothers" chose that particular brand—darkly implying, of course, that a "bad mommy" label should apply to anyone who didn't.

This psychology of selling stuck. We may not be rats, but certainly some of the same principles still apply. While none of us starts scampering down the equivalent of a rat run toward a product during an actress's spiel on self-worth, something connects. Sure, you may want to cover dark roots, but desire extends beyond the obvious: Cosmetics czar Charles Revson may have manufactured beauty products, but what he was really selling, he once said, was "hope in a jar, dreams in a bottle."

It's the message of hope and the promise of dreams fulfilled that takes on so many forms in the media these days. What's changed since the 1950s when Revson first produced different lipsticks to match nail polish each season—thus giving women more opportunities than ever to be fashionable, or equally meaningful, appear passé if they didn't buy the new line—is the increasing use of "selfhood" to sell things. Over the last thirty years, Watson's feel-good theories have morphed into messages that no longer just target the desire to feel good about your product choice. Now, more than ever, they target the desire to feel good about *yourself*, offering objects as the catalyst.

A thousand words.   The power of photography is obviously great, and cameras aren't going away. But it's complicated; while photographic images may provide perspective that may be more realistic than, well, reality, they can trick the eye. And, possibly, trick feelings.

At one time, many groups of people in the world believed (and possibly a few remain who still do) that having their picture taken would steal their soul. However, for most of us in the Western world, photographic images are a daily part of life, telling stories, conveying information, and presenting a finite piece of time or experience that once only words could convey.

Photographic images may bring us closer to something by offering a distanced perspective: Recently, I read about a therapist who helps patients by going over their old family photos to explore how they felt at the time a picture was taken. Another therapist uses photography in her work with her anorexic patients, who, reportedly, gain insight into their condition when viewing a photograph rather than looking in the mirror.

The increasing use of images in the last several decades doesn't necessarily mean that we believe the happy confidence on the faces of actors can be bought. Tell-all magazines about the actors' personal lives prevent wholehearted belief in what we see; "behind-the-scenes" videos explain how special effects happen. But arguably, those images can move into your mind—and make you feel the potential to put yourself in the picture. In an increasingly image-laden environment, the promises of self-esteem through objects would appear to be so real, it's easier than ever to be fooled. Rationally, we know self-esteem comes from within, but the preponderance and immediacy of images may meld internal worthiness with external appearance—which may have an impact on self-perception.

Stress: The new scorecard.   Just as more photographs may affect how we see ourselves, so do more words on what might be, well, wrong. While magazines identified "overpressure" from life that hit housewives, businessmen, and even children as far back as the 1880s, in recent years, stress has come into its own. It's hard to know whether we actually feel more stressed than ever, but clearly, we're paying more attention to it. Stress may be relative, but as an ailment, it ranks right up there with the common cold these days. Since feeling good in your skin is tough when you're completely stressed-out, the message of stress-relief through acquiring stuff has gotten louder than ever. And it's heard; surveys have shown that a majority of American women say they cope with stress by shopping.

Stress is real. And it can certainly make you feel bad. But interestingly, stress is as close to a modern marker of status as anything in our culture. You're stressed because you're busy because you're needed. Because you make a difference. Because you have no time to do all the things that need to get done in your life. Stress, trumpeted as a kind of amorphous, ever-present state that needs changing, may also be a new sort of scorecard.

And stress relief through the acquisition of objects may be a new kind of competition. In an article in the *New York Times*, reporter Julie V. Iovine wrote, not entirely tongue in cheek, "I call it the Competitive Stress Syndrome, whereby the afflicted measure their success in direct ratio to their equally desperate need to relax. For example, a working mother who gets six hours of sleep a night deserves one spa treatment a month; a nursing working mom who survives on four hours rates two spas and a new pair of shoes (no heels!)."

The message that "stress is the enemy but you're a nobody without it" is rampant these days. Being stressed-out is one way to feel deserving, but then, what do you get out of it in the long run? And what does an object—or even a time-consuming visit to the spa—do to actually change the stressors?

Me, me, me.   The stress-progression—and focus on self-rewards for our suffering—over the last decade is only one of the more recent incarnations of a longer-term trend: the All About Me movement. Since the late 1960s, the focus on personal freedom, self-expression, self-improvement, and frank, public self-confession has grown significantly. The old virtue of keeping a stiff upper lip, say, became the misdemeanor of being uptight. The threat of being in "denial"—as opposed to the old idea of not airing dirty laundry, for example, and just shutting up about your problems—began to reign. The motivation to Know Thyself, of course, is laudable. It's just that the all-important Me, the self as macrocosmic, ever-unfulfilled island, has floated into bigger seas than ever.

And that's where Knowing Thyself, and by extension, Loving Thyself, may get translated into Buying for Thyself. Taking care of others morphed into "taking care" of yourself—by buying. More images than ever of purchasable ways to express this newly evolved sense of identity—to oneself and to the rest of the world—effectively illustrated this concept. And seamlessly incorporated into our culture over the last forty-odd years is the growing notion of self-reward, as large as a new boat or as small as a piece of chocolate. You deserve it; never before has the rallying cry of entitlement reached so many, so loudly.

The subtext in the messages of Treat Yourself, Pamper Yourself, and You're Worth It is that Nobody Really Appreciates You But You. Within the answer of objects is the flip side of deserving, the subtle but distinct hiss that says You Stink, You're Not Worth It, You Should Feel Lousy. It may strike at the inner teen, the sullen "adultescent" who surfaces all over these days. In this structure, demonstrating self-worth takes on a self-righteous, defensive posture; its armaments are the number and kinds of things with which you gift yourself.

While it's doubtful that anyone truly confuses self-absorption with self-respect, or self-indulgence with self-worth, the messages may still take root. And whether seeing endless images of people who feel dandy about themselves because they're using a particular product can make us actually feel the need to buy in is questionable. Even so, they can have an impact.

Driven by images, the promises of products imbued with self-worth imply a great, invisible audience that's observing you. Self-esteem isn't just between you and your hair. It's as much about "self" as it is about other people out there, waiting to judge you and your hair as well.

The World Is Watching

Most of us don't move through life in a stupor of self-consciousness, worrying about what other people think of us and our possessions. We don't base our self-worth on whether we've impressed someone else favorably with using a certain caliber of pen in their presence, for example. And despite some of the no-holds-barred, nasty commentary about celebrities' appearance that has preceded televised awards ceremonies in recent years, most people don't run the risk of public ridicule when they step outside.

Still, what other people think of you matters, and there's a strange fascination in hearing a celebrity's appearance get dissected by a cackling commentator. It may play into satisfying a sense of security—hey, even the famously beautiful aren't above scrutiny—but it capitalizes on insecurity as well. Better to hear someone doing it on TV than imagine that they're doing it about you.

And we certainly hear often enough that you *are* your stuff— your inadequacies as well as your successes. Whether anyone else *really* notices or cares is up for debate. The point is the ever-present threat that they might, and that your failings of all sorts will become glaringly obvious to the outside world. Your slips will show, and you will be shamed.

The threat of social retribution for failing to live up to certain material standards has lurked a long time, of course. Although a 1930 print ad for a particular brand of toilet seat now seems nearly laughable in its melodrama, it defined social insecurity that still sells things. With a black-and-white illustration of cloche-wearing ladies at a tea party, the copy spins a horrifying scenario—*people talking behind your back in your own home: "And. . . did you notice the bathroom?* At that moment the hostess re-entered the room. She just barely overheard. But it was more than enough. She began talking about Junior, about bridge, about anything—but like chain lightning her mind reviewed the bathroom. She saw it suddenly as a guest must see it, saw the one detail that positively clamored for criticism. She vowed to change it immediately. . . "

What could be more awful? Then again, is it *possible* that the ladies are discussing this somewhere else—like the facilities at a previously smart restaurant now going downhill? Obviously, the unfortunate heroine of the ad doesn't think so. Sure, it may be a little paranoid to presume that her cruddy old toilet seat merits scorn that translates to personal failure, or for that matter, any attention at all at a social gathering. But then, a little paranoia is the point, isn't it?

Private torment is one thing, but a public display of low self-esteem via an old bathroom seat—or a tacky dress—is about as bad as it gets in a materialized framework. Over the years, that message has, perhaps, gotten a bit less heavy-handed in the telling. But we may be more exposed to it than ever.

How much do Americans care about what others think of them? How does concern about others' judgment affect personality and behavior? It's an issue we've wrestled with for a long time. The 1950 book *The Lonely Crowd*, a "study of the changing American character" by David Riesman, Nathan Glazer, and Reuel Denney, chronicles a perceived shift from an "inner-directed" American character—individuals with a strong internal set of beliefs—to those who are "outer-directed," conformists dependent on and directed by the example and approval of their contemporaries.

The theme continued close to thirty years later in *The Culture of Narcissism*, when Christopher Lasch wrote about "diminishing expectations" manifested in self-absorption, noting that Americans' anxiety about others' opinions of them was greater than in the past. By the late 1990s, a theory on the impact of others on character, personality, and behavior took an even more radical turn: In the prize-winning, controversial book *The Nurture Assumption*, Judith Rich Harris asserts that a child's personality develops through approval or rejection by peers. Forget "good" or "bad" parenting. According to Harris, aside from genes, it's kids' friends that really count when it comes to how they turn out.

Does "fitting in" now direct personality and behavior more than personal ethics or "rugged individualism" identified with the "old days"? Are our characters truly shaped more by the goal of external approval or conformity than, say, seventeenth-century New England Puritans were? It's a tough call. Clearly, however, the issue of conformity and the possible effects of What Other People Think have become subject to more scrutiny over the past five decades.

And not without reason. The growth of the mass media in that time has immeasurably widened the net of "other people" from whom we receive information on social or moral standards and repercussions, for better or worse. It's broadened and amplified the ways we may perceive that someone else is judging who we are by what we own. Delivery of that information, with greater speed and volume than ever before, may position outside approval as a priority for feeling good in one's own skin.

And that self-consciousness can't help but include our possessions. "I'd like to believe that I really don't care what other people think of my apartment or appearance, but I'd be lying if I said it didn't matter," said a woman who recently turned thirty. "But around the time of my birthday it occurred to me that I'd devoted a lot of thought and time in my life to others' approval, and it wasn't making me very happy. It's hard to try to see beyond how other people see you or your stuff, but I'm trying. When I catch myself asking, 'What would they think?' I try to ask myself if it really matters."

Whether the "fragmentation" of the self that Kohut described actually takes shape in a detail of the run-down bathroom or in seeking a piece of approval from an outside audience, it may still get magnified through the lens of materialism. Whether it's a photograph or the view of a critical onlooker, the picture is colored by the filter of the viewer. Creating fullness in the picture of oneself, perhaps, may require something much larger and less finite than a single image or fragments of objects.

And maybe that means reassessing the notion of happiness not as the pursuit of a destination where there's a cheering section, but as something that can be identified, on one's own terms, in one's own day. It's worth considering writer Herman Hesse's notion that "happiness is a how, not a what; a talent, not an object."

Live the Fantasy

The "how" of self-worth and happiness may be a talent that can only be nurtured in moments of reality, but the current climate specializes in a grander scheme: the possibility of living a fantasy by buying what you hope to become.

For a magazine assignment about landscape design, I once interviewed a group of garden designers. Some of their garden "rooms" were lush and fragrant, others spare and almost sculptural. They talked about working with natural boundaries and elements rather than fighting them, and about using native plants in new and interesting ways. They agreed that transformation had limitations: Much as a client in the Pacific Northwest might yearn for a stark desert landscape, it was likely it wasn't going to work.

Working with plants, the landscape designers told me, is also an exercise in working with human nature. Along with asking clients practical questions about things like upkeep, they try to find out how clients could see themselves in the garden once it was finished. "I ask people to tell me their wildest fantasies," said one designer. "Do they secretly want to be an old-time cattle baron, even if they live in a suburb? As a gracious Southern belle receiving callers? As a philosopher in ancient Greece? It tells me more than clients saying they like tulips or hate rhododendrons. Once I understand their dreams, it helps me create a space that helps them live the fantasy."

But can it actually happen? It's pretty darn hard to maintain a fantasy garden, never mind living an image—say, instantly becoming a philosopher simply because your yard gets a few olive trees. But when buying objects is positioned as a way to acquire a new life, you can always try.

A woman who recently broke up with her boyfriend and is unhappy at her work told how it happens: "I see these beautiful wine glasses in a store and suddenly have a long, involved daydream where I see myself giving a party where people admire them. I see myself laughing and saying something witty to the group as I pour a great vintage wine. Oh yes, then I meet some wonderful guy that someone's brought. Actually, I already have plenty of wine glasses, and don't need any more. But at that moment, the new ones are the answer to 'What am I doing with my life?' They kick off a whole scenario in my head, and I end up buying them. And not giving the party. And I'm still asking, 'What am I doing with my life?'"

A lawyer in his forties said, "I just buy stuff out of boredom with myself. When I don't want to engage in my life at the moment, I'll go buy a bunch of CDs. It's immediate gratification to feel less disgusted with myself for things I'm not doing, sort of like going out and getting drunk. Recently, before I start buying, I've tried to pinpoint what I'm avoiding doing instead. It's not really hard to stop yourself when you drag yourself out of the situation and look objectively at what you're doing."

The happy moment at the cashier, when all may still be possible, is certainly seductive. While point of purchase doesn't have to turn into a moment of truth every time you go to the store, "checking out" may sometimes mean more than simply parting with cash. So here's an idea: Before checking out with the dream of expectation in an object, check in with yourself. While spending money certainly comes into play here—is the thing you're buying going to collect dust in your bathroom cabinet, hang, unused in your closet, or end up in the trash in six months, the reason why you ever acquired it long-forgotten?— what's equally important is what you're actually investing in it.

Clearly, one of the most appealing things about objects is the escapist pleasure they may offer; it can certainly take your mind off your fight with your girlfriend to immerse yourself in looking for the perfect pair of pants. Or feel you're doing something about your depressing social life by buying a black-tie outfit for "someday." Focusing on objects is a good way of getting out of feeling something less than pleasant. But it's worth listening for a subtext: What is that feeling telling you about yourself?

The feel-good promises of objects address small, external parts of ourselves, and sometimes they can even help. The lipstick might not change your life, but it may improve your mood momentarily. But the whole self—the one who has good feelings and bad, the one who is unique, the one who is able to experience and learn and grow—may need time to feel, assess, and address the sense of feeling low. The constant jabber of quick-fix/feel-good doesn't allow much room for contemplation or putting things into perspective in your own life.

Nor does it take into account the idea that experiencing that feeling may be part of finding your way out of it. Nearly anyone can pay for hair color because they're "worth it." But only you can pay attention to your own feelings. And so it may be worth engaging in the feeling, knowing that it won't last forever, rather than instantly finding distance from it through an object.

In the early 1990s, Joe Dominguez and Vicki Robin, authors of *Your Money or Your Life,* advised assessing how many real hours of work and "life force" went into a purchase to decide whether something was worth the expense. Making a connection between the time and energy you spend working and the money you spend might do something for personal-savings rates, which have slipped precipitously since the book first appeared. (In fact, according to the Economic Policy Institute, they'd fallen to nothing at all by 1998.) But let's just say, for a moment, that money doesn't matter—and consider, instead, the spending of emotional time and energy on the idea of objects.

It takes just a minute to break the reverie and check in with the whole self you already have, and view the object, well, objectively. What will you change in your feelings about yourself by buying it? What can it do for you that isn't already there in your life? And how does the fantasy of a fabulous future starring the object intrude, perhaps, on what needs some energy now?

If you still want the object, go for it. But it's worth considering the difference between the moment of dreaming about the object and what really happens when you finally possess it. Taking a moment to break the spell of expectation, to quell the internal voice that may link worthiness with purchasing, may help to extricate the self from the object—and find, perhaps, that what you have, even in low moments, may be enough.

Worthiness from Within

Aristotle's idea of happiness is distinct from the fairy-tale notion of Happily Ever After, which persists in the modern myth of Happy All the Time. Happy All the Time implies that something is wrong with you if you have a bad-hair day, if your confidence is shaken by, say, a bad meeting, or if you make a mistake in parenting. Happy All the Time connotes that there is always a solution, a way out of not feeling perfectly content constantly.

The difference here is that Aristotle viewed happiness as an on-going state of worthiness from within, while modern messages of self-esteem through "external regulators" of objects say it can applied like putty to a cracked wall.

Of course, humans can't really be fixed like some home-repair project. Actually feeling worthy is a personal process that involves the whole self, and not a checklist of parts that could use some work. And that process may begin with taking stock of what's already there, not in some fantasy future of self-improvement.

The notion of personal affirmations may have moved into the spoof realm of *Saturday Night Live* skits featuring the character Stuart Smalley who proclaims, "I'm good enough, I'm smart enough, and doggone it, people like me!" but they may merit consideration in an era punctuated by so many external messages that promise you'll feel okay about yourself—if you just consume something else. Okay, so maybe you feel a little foolish standing in front of the mirror telling yourself how wonderful you are every day, but now and then it's worth reminding yourself of what you have in who you are. What's good, beautiful, and impossible to reproduce about you, right now? What qualities do you possess that can't be bought?

The external focus on hiding flaws, righting mistakes, and momentarily enhancing mood with stuff can overwhelm the fact that life (along with your face, body, and anything else that's a focus) has flaws, that humans make mistakes, and that self-esteem may include acceptance of what is, and not what could be. For every personal failing there may not always be an equal and opposite personal success—but surely both exist in all of us.

Feeling complete, then, may come from working to develop a sense of unconditional love toward the self, warts and all, rather than responding to the twin messages of self-hate and hope so continually linked to the act of buying things. As one young woman put it, "I recently realized that the person who I am is who I'm stuck with forever, so I'd better try to like that person."

"The gift of turning forty," said another woman, "was to finally feel comfortable with who I'd become. I spent years beating myself up over things that didn't really matter in the long run. When I finally stopped looking at my life as a series of things to fix and began to understand that my time was limited, I began to feel better."

Joy Postponed

A long time ago, in a toy store in New York, I noticed a small, hand-lettered sign that said, "Don't Postpone Joy." Although I wasn't sure that buying a jumping windup toy—the store specialized in these—was going to deliver joy to my life then and there, the idea stayed with me. Delaying or deciding against a purchase is one thing, but postponing joy is another.

So what's the difference between buying the toy and getting the joy? The answer of objects is limited: You will get happy once you get it. Okay, there's no telling how long it will last, or if it will actually deliver what you seek. On the other hand, joy that comes through the experience of living has no limits.

While much has been said about the declining ability of Americans to delay gratification, I'd argue that faith in ownership of objects actually is an exercise in deferred gratification. If objects are the key that opens the door to good feelings, well, you'd better sit tight until you can get to the mall to obtain those feelings. Finding joy in experience, however, is as close as we can get to immediate gratification—and can be found anywhere, any time.

The word *serendipity* comes from the title of the mid-eighteenth-century fairy tale *The Three Princes of Serendip* by Horace Walpole, whose heroes "were always making discoveries, by accidents and sagacity, of things they were not in quest of." So maybe joy, like those serendipitous discoveries, isn't something you can hunt down or buy. Perhaps it's worth considering this: The potential to feel good in one's own skin may come from believing that one—anyone—is worthy of serendipity. And that it's there to be found.

So how does one go about finding joy? Like the answer of objects, identifying joy is easiest with contrasts. Just as the new pair of shoes may beckon when you feel completely strung out from work, recognition of joy may come in the moment between the darkest hour and the dawn, in the morning after "weeping endureth for the night." After an especially awful day away from home, the way your toddler holds your finger with complete trust can bring on a wave of joy that just hits, nearly physical in its intensity. When you've mourned something, finally laughing again may be a remarkable event. And as a man I know said about simply going outside for the first time after a long, serious illness, "I felt as if I could finally see in color again."

But while the sharp contrasts of difficult experience and joy may make joy more apparent, living with the belief that it is there, regardless of where you may be, may be helpful in finding it. The meaning of objects operates on the idea of how something should be; the finding of joy exchanges that for how something actually is. It's where you find it: "It sounds strange, but I get great pleasure out of an orb spider that's building a web on my porch," a septuagenarian told me. "For a while I thought I should get rid of it, since it's a bit odd to cultivate a large, round web on your front porch. But I realized I look forward to seeing what the spider has done every day. Maybe it's a little weird, but I enjoy it."

The capacity for finding enjoyment in yourself and the world isn't thwarted by our culture, but it's not promoted much, either. But simply enjoying something as it is may be a quality we can cultivate. Despite what we hear constantly, it's possible to relish the ice cream without considering the calories or enjoy the smell of newly cut grass without worrying about how your own lawn looks. Rather than limiting joy, dematerializing enjoyment—and feeling good in one's skin—may mean simply becoming more open to its possibilities.

4

~:~

UNDERSTANDING

Does your husband
misbehave
grunt and grumble
rant and rave?
Shoot the brute some
Burma-Shave.

—1920s ADVERTISEMENT

From the time Mark was twelve until he entered college, conversations with his father deteriorated into arguments over his ripped jeans, body piercings and oversized T-shirts. No matter what they tried to say to each other before the fighting erupted—that the father was proud of his son's excellent grade on a test, that Mark was happy his father had come to his soccer game—the teen-age attire became a wall between them. For five years, "you don't get it" became a refrain for both father and son.

The student who told me this story had the insight, five years later, to understand that his way of dress as a teenager "was my way to be independent. Dad assumed I was rejecting everything he'd worked for." They get along now, he says, but regrets "we wasted all those years fighting about things that didn't really matter. We were both so sure the other was wrong. "

Why are objects so powerful in expressing who we are and what we believe? And why do they get in the way of what we really want to say?

There's no question that objects serve as effective shorthand. Certainly, they can convey economic, social, cultural, and personal information; for years, archeologists have pieced together theories about entire ancient civilizations from the things people have left behind. But while artifacts can tell you about how an individual lived, the objects he valued, and even what he worshiped, they convey little about his character or the quality of his relationships with other people.

That kind of understanding is left to the living. Just as time or new archeological discoveries can change the way we see an artifact—a "lustral bathing chamber" at Knossos once thought to be used for hallowed purification rituals is now believed to just be somebody's bathtub (a wealthy somebody, but still a bathtub)—the meaning of objects is open to interpretation. The room may have lasted intact for millennia, but its meaning moved from the mundane to the sacred and again to the mundane.

Along with beauty, the meaning of objects is in the eye of the beholder: ripped blue jeans, T-shirt, and body piercings can take on powerful, sometimes contradictory messages—rebellious rejection or assertive independence—depending on how you view them. And that meaning, because it seems so direct and powerful and true, may overwhelm what really needs to be said.

Certainly, we value quick and easy communication, and with more ways to communicate than ever, it seems like it should be faster and easier to "get it," especially in relationships we value most. The problem, obviously, is that true understanding or really being understood isn't always quick and easy. And despite increasing numbers of ways to "stay in touch," we may still miss the most important connections.

Which may make us human. Although other living creatures feel, act, and react, and communicate to some extent, we alone can speak, listen, and analyze. And while we can use objects to communicate many things, they're crude substitutes for the nuances in ideas and feelings that we're capable of expressing and sharing. While possessions may speak loudly, they can fail to further real understanding. The language of objects says something, for sure. But it may also make us miss what we need to hear.

Appearances and Deception

As part of a unit about diversity, students in my son's fifth-grade class were asked to write about whether they "prejudged" people before they knew them. Sure, they've been taught that you can't judge a book by its cover, but come on. My son and his friend agreed diversity was a good thing, that accepting "differences" is important, but even in fifth grade, they know that it matters what your "cover" happens to be. It matters that you don't have a dorky haircut or look like your mom still picks out your clothes. Maybe it doesn't matter as much as other things, but it matters.

Of course we prejudge people. It's part of a survival instinct to mentally categorize others based on their appearance and the objects they own. It's a way of creating order, a shortcut.

Appearances may deceive—the prince is actually a pauper, or the frog a prince—but the way someone looks is a starting point.

The movie *Pretty Woman*, the story of a tough but appealing prostitute with a sterling character who captures the heart of her handsome client, is a fairly ridiculous modern fairy tale. But it contains a small nugget of truth: When the streetwalker goes into a snooty Rodeo Drive boutique, she's snubbed by the nasty sales help. Even though she may have an eighteen-karat heart and a lovely face and body, they see only her trashy attire.

Later in the movie, the prostitute returns to the store, dressed in expensive clothes. The salespeople, who of course don't recognize her from her previous visit, are eager to help her. The spunky heroine will have none of this pandering hypocrisy, however. In a scene that's the ultimate revenge fantasy for anyone who's been treated badly based on appearance, she tells the snobbish salesgirl she's not buying—and how the salesgirl lost out big-time on a commission because she was mean.

Ah, the power! But what's really happening here? The prostitute is still a prostitute, albeit with better clothing. The mean salesgirl will no doubt continue to be mean to anyone who looks like a streetwalker. There's a momentary satisfaction in the noble prostitute giving the salesgirl her comeuppance by calling the shots on superficial, unkind judgments. Except that it doesn't really work that way. What's really communicated here is that the prostitute's new finery empowers her to act as nasty as anyone.

And think about the actual objects. A cheap pair of street-walkers' stilettos don't look so different from some of the stilt-like, snakeskin pumps (costing many hundreds of times more) that grace the pages of fashion magazines. The difference between the two pairs of shoes, both designed to say "come hither" (in the words of more genteel times), is not so great. Understanding the distinctions between four-inch heels that scream "floozy" and those expensive heels deemed "fabulous" by tastemakers or trendsetters is part of our cultural lexicon— knowledge accessible to nearly everyone, but known by only a select few.

Most of those differentiators aren't nearly so subtle, of course. Spiked hair and a black-metal nose ring clearly communicate something that's a far cry from a cashmere twinset and pearls. Material goods factor into how the world responds to us and always has throughout history: It's been said that Queen Elizabeth I, whose claim to the throne came under dispute, *needed* a massive number of pearl-encrusted and other elaborate outfits to lend legitimacy to her standing as queen.

Perhaps she needed to communicate something to herself as well. Objects we own may play a part in how we respond to the world. But to what extent? The power of objects to communicate, while always there, may have a larger, more complex vocabulary than ever.

Onward and Upward

It's hard to know exactly how or why we feel pressured to communicate through upscale objects, but it's safe to say we do. And "flaunting it" may be increasingly linked to prestige. We may not believe we can buy status, but, according to *American Demographics* magazine, in 1998 Americans were "more likely to grant status to 20 trended items than they were just two years earlier."

And we're spending more. As Robert Frank points out in *Luxury Fever*, increases in wealth for the superrich have raised the spending stakes for all consumers. Communicating that you are "respectable"—never mind worthy of respect—has gotten more expensive. These days, going upscale with the items you own isn't so much about winning the social or personal communication game as simply staying in it.

Granted, in these logo-laden times, it's tempting to dismiss communication through objects as a simple economic equation: The more you spend on stuff, the more respect you get, and the richer you appear, the more power you have. Certainly, communication through objects may have always involved money. But the recent, meteoric rise of logomania may have as much to do with the promise of something even more special: authenticity.

A handbag that's deemed a "must-have" among fourteen-year-olds can cost upwards of three hundred dollars, and sure, it may be well made or good looking. But it's the distinct designer label that differentiates it from a near-exact replica available from street vendors at one-tenth the price. That label—and perhaps, a few tiny details discernible only to those in the know—is what makes the pricey bag "real."

Running alongside this approach is another kind of authenticity. In recent years, aided by an intensive advertising campaign, one "authentic" approach was all about natural fibers—think of that African-Colonial out-on-safari-in-pristine-linen look. Now, *there* was ultimate fantasy presented as "real"—you might spend the day traveling the veldt, but you'd always look bandbox fresh in your natural-fiber designer clothing, since of course you have a laundress or houseboy to iron your clothes, even when stalking rhinos!

It's likely that the increasing number of messages about the importance of "genuine" articles has enlarged the number of people who know the difference between the branded article and knockoffs. The "identity" and aura of authenticity linked to an object, of course, don't change the item itself, or what it does for you. But the focus on communication conveyed through something "real" versus a "fake" may have grown in recent years. While authenticity and honesty of actual communication between two people doesn't have a lot to do with the "authenticity" of a handbag or a jacket, it may appear, increasingly, that it does.

Understanding and the Emperor's New Clothes

We can confuse a yearning for something "real" that transcends possessions with *owning* possessions. And fulfilling the yearning for authentic understanding between people can get translated into swapping superficial symbols—or acquiring similar objects.

The topsy-turvy story of the prince and the pauper changing stations in life by exchanging clothes is an old one. And over the last half-century, the desire for communication by swapping objects has played out in real life: Wishing to become one with "the people," the rich college student shed the loafers and donned work boots. The styles of mostly black urban neighborhoods have flowed out to kids in predominantly white, affluent suburbs; conversely, the old logos of establishment luxury took to the streets. The casual attire of Internet innovators is embraced in formerly buttoned-down Wall Street boardrooms.

The emperor's new clothes? Perhaps. Imitation, however, is the sincerest form of flattery, and the symbols of understanding are strong. Still, the situation begs analysis: Did the college student's new costume result in his gaining any knowledge—say, actually having a conversation—with people who might not be able to afford to go to college? Does the curiosity and admiration from afar that appears in the swapping of clothes styles among kids lead to any real cultural exchange? Does the newly tie-less Wall Streeter gain insight—or financial rewards—by dressing like people who never dressed for success and got rich anyway, by taking lucky risks at the right time?

It's possible that Marie Antoinette really yearned for some sort of communion with those she perceived as the simple but happy poor. And she may have taken great pleasure in leaving the opulent Hall of Mirrors at the Palace of Versailles and playing peasant by frolicking in the clothes of a milkmaid. But since she ended up beheaded, what did it get her in terms of really understanding or communicating with her subjects?

Okay, you could counter the sad fate of Marie Antoinette with the triumph of Elizabeth I, so there's more to communication than clothing. And while the beheading block doesn't await those who buy into the notion that clothes or other objects always make the man (or woman), there's still a loss involved: Faith in dressing up (or down) may distract us from what actually needs to be said or done.

Or, perhaps, *heard*. Reducing ideas, feelings, or an actual exchange to perceptions of possessions is certainly easier than looking further. Avoiding prejudging, as the fifth-grade curriculum says, may make the world a better place. But especially now, it's easier said than done. Still, there's a payoff that's anything but altruistic to rethinking judgments based on objects. Frankly, it's selfish: You have a lot to gain.

The divisions that objects create may blind: When you see only the expensive suit, you miss the opportunity to learn more about the person as a person, not just as a rich guy. When you allow a person's objects to become mediator and microphone, what you hear may be loud, but it may also be flat, atonal, or distorted, missing the nuances, depth of insight, and satisfaction of actual understanding.

The Grand Gesture

It's a bird! It's a plane! Wait, is it Superman? No. . . it's the obnoxious guy/class nerd/angry young man of the old days arriving at your high school reunion in a private helicopter!

He's rich now. He's important. He's going to show everyone how much he's changed.

But it doesn't have to be the guy in the helicopter. It can also be the good-natured overweight girl who never had a boyfriend—who's now lost fifty pounds, is wearing an expensive pair of tight leather pants, and may be considerably less good-natured now than in the past.

The Grand Gesture is the stuff of cliché, fantasy, and daydreams. And since it's fantasy, the sky's the limit: you can communicate anything you want and the people you want to reach will listen to exactly what you say. You can plan the looks of awe and surprise on their faces, plot their attempts to get the attention of one who is now so transformed, and spin some stunning put-downs of those who once hurt you. Or perhaps, in your reverie, you rise above all that and even plan your gracious forgiveness of those who didn't recognize your gifts in the past. Nonetheless, you'll show them now.

So what is the guy in the helicopter or the girl in the leather pants really trying to say? Maybe nothing at all. On the other hand, maybe their appearance is intended to signify empowerment and change, an attempt to show depth—see how much I've grown? Perhaps it conveys a desire to communicate, engage, be understood on one's own terms as evidenced through objects. And it may show that a person cares—perhaps desperately—what other people think of them.

And there lies the conflict: Anyone could tell you that true communication doesn't exist on a single set of terms. Enticing though it may be, other people don't respond like actors in a set play. Especially to a script carefully structured by a single mind.

Of course, the Grand Gesture isn't limited to solitary daydreams of grandeur. Often, it involves another person or a larger audience. But it always involves objects.

Which may end up projecting something other than the intended message. As one woman noted, "My husband and I had been working long hours, we were struggling with finances, and things were pretty tense. When my birthday came around, he presented me with a very expensive jacket, which we couldn't afford and I didn't need. I didn't want to be ungrateful, but it made me angry. It was as if he thought that all the hours of not talking about things and my worries about money would somehow go away if he gave me that jacket. I felt like he was trying to buy me off. I guess it was supposed to make everything all better, but it only made things worse."

Who knows what her husband actually intended? Despite the constant messages we receive on communicating your innermost feeling through objects, they're subject to misinterpretation. The Grand Gesture can become a potent symbol that something more meaningful is still missing. The danger in allowing objects to speak for you is that they may not convey what you actually intend to say.

In the O. Henry story, "The Gift of the Magi," a husband and wife, low on money, want to give each other elaborate presents. In a classic case of missed communication and objects, she cuts and sells her hair to buy him a watch fob. He sells his watch to buy her a pair of fancy hair combs. Oops.

It's two Grand Gestures gone awry, and they point up the power of intent and of objects. The couple in the story adore each other, and are eager to do whatever it takes to buy something to prove it. Sure, the depth of their passion remains, despite the useless gifts. But while surprises are nice, wouldn't it have made more sense for them to try to make their feelings known, not in a gesture, but in a way that was, perhaps, less grand but more meaningful?

Extracting Payment

Almost from birth, we learn the power of objects not only to communicate, but to motivate. If you're a good girl, you get a cookie. If you're bad, a toy gets taken away. And there's probably not a parent alive who hasn't, at least once, used threats or bribes with objects to produce desired behavior.

After all, it's pretty tough to reason with a two-year-old. The momentary withholding or rewarding of something concrete sends a stronger signal, at times, than an hour's worth of reasoning or discussion of feelings. The law gets laid down; the consequences are spelled out. You get what you want by behaving in the right way; what you want is taken away if you don't.

Cause and effect with objects as an intermediary is ingrained in us early on; extrinsic rewards and threats continue throughout life. But while a system of bribery and threats using objects may work on occasion to get a toddler to behave better, it doesn't do much to promote genuine understanding between two people.

Objects may motivate. But what happens when they're used as weapons?

I once overheard a conversation between a father and his two children about their grades. The father was disappointed in his children's less-than-stellar showing at school, lecturing his kids on the importance of getting good grades. Then he proposed a solution. For every "A" they received, they would get an expensive toy; a "C" or lower would result in something being taken away. He never asked his children why they hadn't done well; perhaps he didn't want to know. He never discussed his feelings about learning or asked them theirs. It appeared the father believed it was enough to simply make a threat and offer a bounty for the desired results.

But what was he really saying to them? And what happens when the toy isn't enough to motivate? Or when the threat of withholding objects doesn't work? What's left?

One answer came to me a few years ago, when an acquaintance was giving me a tour of her house. When we got to the master bedroom, I admired a fine quilt on the bed. "Oh, that has a story," she said slyly. "I never would have spent so much money, but one day I was furious at my husband and wanted to do something to get him back. I went out looking for the most expensive thing I could find, because I knew it would make him angry."

Yikes! The symbolism of anger and revenge spread across the marital bed was a little heavy for me, and I wasn't sure I wanted to know any more. But my curiosity got the better of me, and I casually asked if the argument ever got worked out. "Not really," she said. "It's still the same old thing, over and over. I think about it sometimes when I make my bed. But the quilt's beautiful, isn't it?"

Okay, so some might find it somewhat difficult to sleep with something that was a constant reminder of marital discord, but then, to each their own. Still, the conversation raised the question of communication and understanding through objects: Clearly, the bedspread could continue to communicate the spirit in which it was bought. My acquaintance had made her symbolic bed—her anger and perhaps the thrill of some sort of vengeful victory for cover—and now, apparently, she could sleep in it.

When objects become instruments of emotional extortion, who wins? I've heard justifiably exasperated parents say, "As long as my teenager lives in my house, they'll do what I want them to do." Theoretically, this makes some sense. On the other hand, where is a disobedient fifteen-year-old going to go if you kick them out? As a parent, of course, you probably don't want to think of your child—no matter how irritating or destructive—ending up on the streets. So something to consider, instead of the power of objects, is what you really hope to accomplish. Which may come only in working on ways to try to understand what someone else wants as well.

The symbolic power of objects, while great, is finite: Though a bouquet of roses may help heal and a bedspread may help keep bad feelings afloat, ultimately, it's likely these things can't provide deeper understanding of either. The power of working to understand another person, however, is infinite, offering real possibility for communication and change.

Just as one man's weed is another man's wildflower, individuals bring entirely different meanings to possessions. It's hard to move beyond weed, wildflower, or any other definition to simply experience the plant itself. And it's hard to get past the need to insist that your own definition is the only one that's right. But ultimately, putting aside the desire to be heard may be the way we can understand.

I once heard about an exercise from a woman who was training to become a peer counselor to older people dealing with the aging process. In order to become better listeners, the people who participated in the training session teamed up and took turns talking. For five minutes, one person had to keep talking about a challenge or setback in their life; the other person could use nonverbal communication, but say nothing. In short, the person listening had to shut up, withholding comments, judgments, or any other response.

It wasn't easy, the woman told me. We are accustomed to observing, hearing, processing—and rapidly responding with opinions framed by our own experiences. We are used to interaction and interruption. Those five minutes, she said, stretched on for a long time, both when she listened and when she spoke.

In real life, of course, we can't give anyone else a gag order. We can't force another person to keep talking. But we can try to understand. What do you want from a relationship? "Listen," an old Cherokee saying goes, "or your tongue will make you deaf." If it's worth pursuing or preserving, then it may be worth, well, shutting up and listening.

Form versus Content

A few years ago, the holiday issue of a magazine featuring how-tos for "The Best Christmas Ever" lay open on my kitchen table. As I remember it, "Giving Guests a Warm Welcome" was the title of the feature that burbled on about showing people how much you care about them during the holiday season. In several glossy photographs, happy, relaxed, good-looking people gathered around a bounteous table with a centerpiece comprised of tiny pine cones that the magazine described as "simple to make and beautiful, too!" In the pictures, the model "mom" (all of nineteen in real life, no doubt) glowed. The kids—immaculate in velvet—were in soft focus somewhere in the background. And, in those photos, the attractive "guests" looked like they had never had such a good time.

This was a few years ago, on the night before a holiday party I was throwing. It was two A.M., and my kids and husband were asleep. And what was I doing? After spending hours cooking, I was staring at the magazine and attempting to make that centerpiece, which, sleep-deprived and intoxicated by all those pictures, I'd somehow decided was essential to the success of my party. Forget that I was probably going to be exhausted for the real event, and would bear little, if any, resemblance to the model "hostess-mom" in the pictures. Forget that my kids would probably be in loud, sharp focus at the party, given the fact that they were real children. And forget that my guests might or might not notice the centerpiece or that they might not appear as delighted as those in the photos—but could still have a good time.

None of that crossed my mind at the time. Here's what did: I wanted that party in the magazine to be mine. I wanted to be in that picture, too, showing everyone how much I cared. And I decided that somehow the effort I was putting into the center-piece was going to make that happen. But "simple and beauti-ful" wasn't coming out that way at all. The pine cones just weren't sticking to the foam balls; the floor was littered with them. But darn it, I was determined to have that centerpiece.

It was when I looked up and got a glimpse in myself in a mir-ror that I had something that was as close to an epiphany as I've ever experienced. There I was, sticky hands wielding a glue gun, with part of a pine cone stuck firmly to my hair. My eyes were bloodshot, gleaming with mad intensity. I looked crazy, I thought to myself tiredly. I *am* crazy. Why am I doing this?

With that glimpse, I got a grip. Within minutes I'd thrown out the magazine and foam balls, swept up most of the pine cones, put away the glue gun, and gone to bed. It was a good feeling.

As for the party, well, the kids were loud and got smeared with chocolate. There were a couple of pine cones under the table. But the food was pretty good, and there was enough of it. The centerpiece was a potted poinsettia that nobody noticed. The guests talked to each other. People laughed. The party didn't turn out like the magazine photographs. It was better.

❧   ❧   ❧

A justice of the peace I know once paraphrased Tolstoy: Just as all happy families are the same, all happy weddings are alike. It's the unhappy ones that are unhappy in their own ways. And, she continued, the location, the dress, the menu, the flowers, and whatever else went into the event made not a bit of difference: Either the wedding was going to be a joyous celebration, or it wasn't. It all depended on the spirit of all involved.

Who hasn't been to a social gathering where everything looked perfect, where the food was fantastic, where things were beautifully organized—except that, for some reason, it wasn't much fun at all? And then there's the other side: The gathering among friends and strangers that just *works*, regardless of overcooked chicken, awful wine, and a fallen cake. What makes these two situations so different? Perhaps, as the justice of the peace pointed out, the hosts and the guests come to the event in a different spirit. And perhaps what's communicated between people at these gatherings makes all the difference.

The rising costs and increasingly elaborate nature of weddings and other social and religious events in recent years may be a simple reflection of many years of a strong economy. And the recent focus on material aspects of entertaining—the more time, money, and attention lavished on the event, the better, say the Prophets of Profit—may certainly enhance a setting, but how much can they enhance the experience of being with other people? As one prospective father of the bride put it, "How much of a difference can a color-coordinated Port-A-Potty really make?"

Of course, in the past, most people probably weren't likely to throw down a bunch of TV dinners when company came over, any more than they are now. And while we don't live in the days of the Roman Empire, when so many elaborate courses of lark's tongues and honeyed eels were served at lavish feasts that guests used a *vomitorium* so they could return to eat even more, the messages we receive these days about gracious entertaining reflect a similar spirit of consumption. It is form— the not-to-be-outdone food, the magnificent place cards, the clever candle-and-flower arrangement in the bathroom, the surprise gift to take home at the end—that we hear about ad nauseum.

The objects involved in the ways people get together with others *can* communicate caring and other attributes. And yes, it's generally more pleasant to have good food than bad, to see a pretty table instead of one covered with crumbs, to feel that someone has made an effort in having you to their house as opposed to feeling that you're an afterthought or obligation. Objects can and do say some of these things. Still, if you've ever been to an awful social event, you know there's a difference between form and content; it doesn't matter how many napkin swans you make if the guests aren't interested in connecting with each other with some level of understanding. It doesn't matter whether people look like models if they don't talk to each other.

Time is precious. Energy is limited. It's probably no coincidence that entertaining at home is on the decline, which some social commentators view as evidence of an era of eroding human connections. Whether you believe that idea or not, nearly everyone still has social obligations that require both time and energy, even if we don't always feel like expending it. And since everyone would rather throw a good party than a bad one, the issue here is separating "they had us to a fancy shindig so we have to have them to a fancy shindig, too" from building relationships that matter more.

That's not to say that you need to dump every well-meaning bore in your life or serve take-out pizza at every social gathering. But examining where form may intrude on content when it comes to social gatherings and relationships may help us evaluate what's most important—and what might be worth giving up.

How much do you get out of the effort you put into specific relationships and social interactions? Which are based on form, and which are based on content of communication? Since all relationships with other people require energy, it's worth taking a look at the returns.

Of course, we can't predict how an event will turn out, regardless how much effort or money we spend. But we can ask what's, well, enough.

It's not easy these days. Rachel, planning her daughter's bat mitzvah, said, "I want to do something simple and meaningful. It's a religious ceremony, after all. But among the people we know, the focus at these events seems to be 'can you top this' in entertainment. I don't want to have a three-ring circus, and can't really afford it, but I don't want my daughter to feel left out, either."

Sorting through desires isn't easy. The easy answer—and pressure—of form can take precedence over something that is worth more. And so what these decisions come down to is motivation and intent. Like the moment that hit as I wielded my glue gun in the wee hours one morning, it may be helpful to step back for a minute and ask some basic questions: Why am I really doing this? And what am I trying to say?

Values of Understanding

Before it even started, our Sunday evening family board game was interrupted; the phone rang, and I got into a long, involved conversation. Our ten-year-old wandered off to see who was on-line on the computer upstairs, and the seven-year-old put on a video. My husband, seeing that the phone conversation wasn't going to end quickly, flicked open his laptop to get some e-mails for work out of the way. All of us ended up alone in separate rooms, communicating or communing in our own way. A half hour later, we were still there.

So much for family time. Even if it doesn't happen in everyone's house the way it did that evening in mine, the technological advances of the last twenty years have impacted the ways we communicate with the world, which may intrude on the time we spend communicating with the people we value most.

Of course, the Internet means you can communicate with far-flung relatives, along with meeting strangers in chat rooms. And while answering the phone just as you're about to do something with your kids may be dumb, it isn't a crime. But the immediacy and urgency of the various ways we now communicate—because we *can,* using our objects—may overwhelm other, more important priorities.

Understanding another person, along with being understood by them, is, of course, a process that requires time. This is not to say that the communication possibilities that technology now offers—unimaginable even a decade ago—are evil, necessary or not. They're now simply part of our lives. But their reach may extend into our lives far beyond the obnoxious guy yelling into his cell phone at the beach. They may beckon, offering a solitary distraction with a machine, that's sometimes a lot easier than actually communicating with another person who may be sitting in the same room.

"Communication" may be instantaneous these days through a variety of objects, but understanding and feeling understood involves time, energy, and, well, commitment. And perhaps that comes back to the question "Why am I really doing this?" whether that means arguing with your kid about his clothes, making a decision about someone based on appearance, or placing faith in an object to speak for you.

The story of our four family members, each in their own techno-space instead of talking to each other, is, perhaps, an apt metaphor for where all kinds of objects intrude on authentic understanding. Each person can retreat into their own space. Each can fulfill their own desires, on their own terms. Each can maintain that they are "right." And, with each withdrawing in their own cocoon, no exchange of ideas or feelings can occur between them.

So maybe a step in working on actual communication that leads to understanding between people comes from removing the metaphor of objects from the picture. Sure, this might mean developing a kind of consciousness about what one actually wants to make a priority. Say, deciding that on a future Sunday, the phone could go unanswered, the computers and video would stay turned off, and we'd actually sit down and spend some time together. And sticking to it.

But working on developing understanding may also mean a kind of turnoff in ourselves and our desire to be understood or be right. The values of acceptance and forbearance aren't pushed much in a materialism-driven environment. The notion of putting yourself—and your burning desire to be understood—on the back burner for a moment probably isn't a super strategy to sell stuff. But it may hold the kind of power that can help us have what we really want.

The desire to understand may involve dropping belief in the megaphone of objects in order to actually hear what a person has to say. It may require questioning whether reciprocating with an object—or many, as in entertaining—is essential to making relationships that matter. And it may mean abandoning the personal desire to make a point, give an opinion, or push an agenda for the greater goal of working to understand someone else.

Does this mean that understanding means becoming a doormat, that communication involves giving in on every disagreement? Does it mean never saying anything when your kid gets a bad grade or is dressed inappropriately? Of course not. But placing the priority of understanding above all else by attempting to listen to and validate another person—as opposed to using objects to communicate to or for us—may be worth the action.

This happened recently to a man I'll call Richard when he recently found himself seated on a commuter flight next to Tom, whom he'd known twenty years earlier.

The two men had gone to both high school and college together. For those eight years, they'd played on the same tennis team, spending many hours practicing and riding buses together to tournaments. Both excellent players and fierce competitors, throughout those years the men had alternated between the number-one and number-two positions on their team. Despite the large amount of time they spent together, and some other shared interests, they never quite became friends. Still, they had a history together, and greeted each other cordially enough when they saw each other that day on the plane.

Soon after they started talking, however, Richard said the conversation turned into the verbal equivalent of a competitive tennis match. Instead of a lofty serve, it started with Tom telling Richard about his huge new house. Richard then returned with a comment about the new pool he was building. Tom then angled for a point by dropping the name of a new car he'd just bought. Richard blocked it with the mention of the more expensive car he was about to buy. And so on.

It could have continued that way, becoming an irritating, inescapable conversation—they were stuck on a plane together, after all. But something remarkable happened, Richard said. As Tom was starting to describe his son's athletic achievements, he stopped himself midsentence. And then said, "Why am I doing this? Why am I bragging to you? We've known each other since we were fourteen, and we went through a lot together. We don't have to do this with each other."

For a minute, said Richard, he was stunned. And then he agreed. Instead of continuing to see Tom as a man who was still his competitor, he saw the boy who had struggled with the same issues that he did. And instead of warily continuing the old competition with what they now owned, they talked about the challenges of work and family in their lives—the issues, not objects, they now had in common.

It wasn't a grand gesture. It wasn't a big deal. But it was a small, sincere effort that prompted deeper communication in this situation. The plane landed and the two men parted, wishing each other good luck, said Richard. And they actually meant it.

5

⌣⋱⌣

BELONGING

They are the we of me. . .

—CARSON MCCULLERS, *THE MEMBER OF THE WEDDING*

I'm channel surfing and land on Ashley, who stands before me, smiling in a long leather trench coat. In the background, the patter of the women's chatter about it is nonstop. It's so soft and flattering, they say, that "all the management women have this coat." Ashley keeps smiling and does a little twirl as the women giggle that they're having so much *fun*. Their phone lines are just going crazy on this one—they're gonna run out, they squeal. "It's an essential," says one of the women. "In two seconds you can change your wardrobe," says the other. Join us, the women urge. It'll be a special secret just between us girls that you didn't spend a fortune on this fabulous item. Don't get mauled at the mall. Call now.

Click. The two fellows are guys' guys, and they're talking man-to-man about the collectible sword collection before them. You'd expect to pay a lot more for a dragon-headed sword with this mirror sheen, says one of the guys. The other nods vigorously, adding that you get five quality swords for

what you might pay for just one in a retail store. "I got this collection at home and when my buddies come over to watch foot-
ball, they can't stop looking at it," he chuckles. "You could even
buy the set and give one or two as gifts. My brother's gettin'
one from me," says the other guy. You can be part of this great
deal. But hurry—call now.

Click. The man and woman sitting cozily on the couch speak
in reverential tones, a cross between golf tournament announc-
ers and museum docents. In the background, a fire crackles
merrily; in front of the pair, on a low table, sits a mass-produced porcelain figurine. Club members have known about the
quality of this porcelain for a long time, the woman murmurs.
The man lovingly caresses the figurine, saying that collectors
will be thrilled that this very special item has been reissued, but
for a limited time only. The churchy tone of this chat is broken
for a moment—they have a phone call. It's someone saying how
much she loves the figurine, and how she's buying it right now.
She's been a club member now for twenty years, along with
some of her girlfriends. "That's so special," says the woman on
the couch, her eyes shining. "Won't you join us?" she asks the
audience, as if extending an invitation for high tea. "Call now."

How long had I been sitting there, clicking between these
people hawking stuff? Five minutes? Ten minutes? An hour?
I'm mesmerized by the Leather Ladies and the Sword Sellers
and the Porcelain Club committee of two. They speak with such
assurance. They have so much to say. And it's not just about the
parade of objects before them. They're talking about becoming
part of something big. They're talking about belonging.

❈   ❈   ❈

It's seductive. But once I tear myself away from the television and start to think again, I realize it reminds me of other messages I've heard recently. Like the one about a "place where we are free to be ourselves, a virtual world where there's no bull and no boundaries." According to one tagline accompanying photographs of happy people in this magical world, "nobody leaves here a stranger." "Welcome home," says another tagline.

Okay, it's just a message on a matchbook, but you can almost feel the embrace of open arms, reading about the Winston Racing Nation. According to the wisdom of that mythical place, happy celebrants "let freedom roar." And you, too, can join by calling an 800 number.

Imagine—authenticity with no limits, acceptance with no responsibility, unity in diversity, and freedom of expression any old way you please. Sounds pretty great, doesn't it?

This place, like so many these days, doesn't actually exist, despite the real-sounding racing car revving in the background when you phone in. But that doesn't mean that it wouldn't be cool to *belong*. And at least you can get the gear that enables you to be part of such an extraordinarily inclusive yet independent-minded community!

The promise of belonging is potent, as powerful as a magic wand that will do away with loneliness or alienation with a flick of the wrist. But even the amazing, modern-day wizard Harry Potter, who finally finds a place to belong at Hogwart's School of Wizardry, can't do that. And while a perfect balance of belonging—the place where "come as you are" and conformity never butt heads—may exist in some mythical Nation, it's a lot tougher to strike in our own.

In 1845, when Alexis de Tocqueville published *Democracy in America*, he wrote about the dangers of a society where everyone was presumed to be equal. Aristocracies and ironclad class structures had their problems, he assented. But at least everyone knew their place. For better or worse, they knew they *belonged*.

Without such a structure, the Frenchman declared, "tyranny of the majority" ruled Americans, which was as bad as any despot who silenced diverse or dissenting ideas. Belonging was not a birthright but a burden, he said, in an environment where "public favour seems as necessary as the air we breathe, and to live at variance with the multitude is, as it were, not to live. The multitude requires no laws to coerce those who think not like itself: public disapprobation is enough; a sense of their loneliness and impotence overtakes them and drives them to despair."

Neither Tocqueville nor other European writers were always so grim in discussing America. Still, it didn't exactly flatter citizens of an independent new country to imply that freedom from old restrictions meant sheeplike subservience to public opinion. Or to be told, as far as future cultural accomplishments went, "there can be no literary genius without freedom of opinion, and freedom of opinion does not exist in America."

More than two hundred years later, Tocqueville's questions on whether majority rule "tyrannizes" independence is still debated. And the human desire to belong—to be part of something larger than oneself, to be wholly accepted for membership—persists.

As Tocqueville observed, knowing one's place isn't always easy. The open-ended idea of democracy also meant, he wrote, that Americans "never stop thinking of all the good things they have not yet got." Social and economic mobility is an important and dynamic characteristic of American life, of course. But in a new environment, built on the idea that all was possible for anyone, a sense of belonging perhaps became tinged with an ever-present longing for something else. Or, as Groucho Marx remarked, "I don't care to belong to a club that accepts people like me as members."

Membership, goes the credit-card ad, has its privileges. And it may have an increasing price. According to a report in the *Federal Reserve Bulletin* on credit-card use over the last thirty years, revolving consumer-credit grew from $2 billion to about $626 billion between 1970 and 2000. The majority of credit-card holders now carry an unpaid balance compared to 37 percent in 1970; the typical American family now carries more than $4,000 in credit-card debt.

While owing money on credit cards doesn't necessarily mean that people are rushing to purchase stuff as a way of belonging, there may be a connection. As David Brooks points out in *Bobos in Paradise: The New Upper Class and How They Got There,* what constitutes "membership" has gotten shaken up in the last forty-odd years. The old guard is gone, he asserts, and a group that he calls Bobos, or Bourgeois Bohemians, now runs things, merging countercultural, arty attitudes of the 1960s with the drive and acquisitiveness of the 1980s and beyond. With other cultural changes—"genteel poverty" has become an oxymoron these days—the new "establishment" has needed to establish itself. That's where consumption comes in.

Bobos acquire objects as a way of belonging to something higher-minded, important, worthwhile, asserts Brooks. Forget old ideas of scrabbling for status and upward mobility: people now may not be charging stuff because they feel pressure to conform, but because they are *choosing* to belong to something that object represents.

And the heck with the cost. The message that a sense of belonging—a choice, not a tyranny—can be bought, not born or made, is big these days. Conveniently omitting the notion that one actually has to *do* something to actually be a part of, say, a community, family or political movement, the sense of easy belonging promised by possessions is as large as spiritual oneness with the universe, or as small as, say, the warmth of an intimate circle of friends. But how far can it go in creating a sense of being part of "we" that's real?

Where You Should Be Now

Across time and cultures, *belongings* have always been part of *belonging*. Only ancient Mayan royalty could wear jaguar skins. Members of early trade guilds had both the obligation and right to wear distinctive clothing. Sumptuary laws through history—from ancient Hawaii to ancient Rome, where only senators were permitted to wear purple bands on their togas—distinguished belonging to a particular group.

Or exclusion from one. As William Manchester writes of medieval Europe in *A World Lit Only by Fire*, "Lepers were required to wear gray coats and red hats, the skirts of prostitutes had to be scarlet, public penitents wore white robes, released heretics carried crosses sewn on both sides of their chests—you were expected to pray as you passed them—and the breast of every Jew, as stipulated by law, bore a huge yellow circle." Years later, distinctions through objects have come up again in fiction and fact: Students still read about Hester Prynne's scarlet "A," and the yellow stars European Jews were required to wear under Nazi rule are powerful reminders of forced "belonging" (or social exclusion, or worse) through objects.

In recent years, possession and display of objects has grown to increasingly encompass aspiration. Maybe you could always "better" your place in the world by buying things, but we've never heard about it quite so much. How come?

The Nameless Problem

In 1963, when Betty Friedan published *The Feminine Mystique*, she examined "the problem that has no name"—women's discontent, if not despair, in the glorified image of housewives in the 1950s. According to Friedan, the "feminine mystique" pushed by the media equated being feminine with utter fulfillment in housekeeping and being a wife and mother. And in buying stuff to better fulfill these roles.

This strictly defined measure of womanhood—there was something *wrong*, even *mannish* with you if you didn't embrace this ideal, or, say, didn't skip with joy over a new type of cleanser—left a lot of women wondering what they were missing. And feeling, as Friedan points out, enormous relief in realizing they were not alone in hating to iron.

Friedan's work galvanized a generation of women—and plenty of men, too. Within a decade the image of desirable womanhood switched from Happy Homemaker to Fulfilled

Worker. Aided by the media, the role of ever-cheerful caregiver, cleaner and cook transformed into something else altogether; the new ideal gal had endless fun working at a stimulating and lucrative job outside the home.

Forget a sense of belonging or satisfaction in the old hearthside ways: members of the new club dressed for success and found themselves elsewhere. Hearth-keeper Hestia got shunted off to the side somewhere, fleet-footed Hermes swooped in, feminized in a floppy bow tie. So what about the demands of the kids who still needed to get fed, the spouse who needed attention, or the house that still needed upkeep? Why, you could have it all!

"Having it all" widened the net on must-have objects, since it synthesized ultrafulfillment in all aspects of life: exciting careers; nurtured, always-happy children; never-sticky kitchen floors; perfect marital relationships; and significant time for yourself. Not unlike belonging to the archetypal Happy Housewife brigade, being part of the "having it all" crew meant never feeling resentful or guilty or exhausted, never questioning the quality of the "all" that you had, since you could always buy wash-and-wear clothing or something else to fill in for your failings—or provide even deeper fulfillment.

The new, absolute answers didn't really pan out any more than the ones they had supplanted. Sadly, real life intrudes on the ideal. Having it all may be super in theory, except when the wash-and-wear clothes have to be washed or the baby-sitter doesn't show. Or when the only "fulfilling" aspect of the job is getting the paycheck. Or when the realistic choice isn't in working or not, but between missing your child's recital or skipping an important meeting.

Recently, a successful television producer and mother, pulled by many demands on her time, said something eerily reminiscent of comments Friedan collected more than forty years ago. "We were sold a bill of goods," she said flatly, "and my friends and I bought right into it, along with the lifestyle that it could buy. I enjoy my work, I like having a nice house, and I love my kids, and don't have enough time or energy to do any of it well. It was all supposed to be so easy, fun and fulfilling, but every day I feel I'm missing something."

A "problem that has no name" remains, and it's not limited to debates over women's roles or social rules. It's not even limited to women. (Think of the conflicting demands and current images of Ideal Guy. He's a caring, in-shape husband, involved father, and a big-time breadwinner, to boot.) But certainly it's still about finding a center where individual yearnings and the feeling of belonging can meet. It's about the promise of an answer, a key to the place where others like you are dancing on greener grass. And the gnawing desire to join them.

But where is the greener grass? How is belonging through ideas and action, however flawed or unrealistic, separate from belonging by owning something? Wanting the same things— contentment with one's family, work that's meaningful, relationships that deliver joy—has, perhaps, gotten translated into wanting the same "things."

Objectification/Personification

The message of fulfilled belonging offered by objects isn't new, but media coverage of acquisition—and what it can do for you—has never been quite so central, either. Entire magazines are now devoted to shopping. Breathless accounts of new gadgets, cosmetics, apparel, and other objects are increasingly positioned as "news you can use."

Magazines and other media can't tell the whole story of individual hopes, dreams, or feelings, but they can serve as cultural barometers, providing a space where consumers of information may see themselves. Naturally enough, "news you can use" attempts to create and reach a "family" or "community" of readers or viewers.

These days, in both news stories and entertainment, high-wattage details of objects shed light on belonging to an inner circle of success or happiness. A story about a business tycoon now isn't complete without drooling mention of the size of his boat or house or jet. An entire episode of the television show *Sex in the City* is devoted to the dogged pursuit of a "real" designer bag at a discount. A piece of short fiction in a recent fashion magazine is chitchat between two women featuring a laundry list of upscale brand names—with no discernible plot, character, or, it seems, purpose. (The subtext, I guess, is that if you're truly a reader in the know, the brand names themselves will say something to you.)

Increasingly, we see and read about the personification of objects and objectification of people. And in more ways than ever, we hear it, too: Terms once used exclusively for material items are now applied to humans. Think of a "high-maintenance" significant other or a "wide-bandwidth" colleague. Consider the desirable "cuts" of muscles, a "six-pack" stomach, or "rack" of a woman's chest, along with "hookup" as a euphemism for sex. The technological metaphors continue with the derisive noun "wetware" (a term that means messily unpredictable humans, as opposed to dependable, reproducible hardware and software) and the term "PEBCAC" ("problem exists between chair and computer"), which also describes dumb, human failure to work with—or live up to—standards set by machines. These terms indicate that the lines between objects and people may be more blurred, at least semantically. (And sometimes obnoxiously: One man I interviewed declared that women should marry young because they have a shorter "shelf life" than men.)

Does this focus on objects or objectification signify something deeper? It's tough to know. But it may introduce a disconcerting idea: What you *don't* own blocks membership from who you want to be.

Ownership as Progress

While belonging isn't always about paying dues, in the current climate it seems always to have a price. The Soccer Mom drives a minivan. The Popular Girl has the brand-name top. The Successful Executive has this year's teeny tiny cell phone. And People Who Have Made It use extralight laptop computers on trains, or preferably, planes. Possessions aren't just props, they're characters.

In this setup, further acquisition marks progress in belonging, a kind of growth that might be measured, say, in dollars or square feet. As one woman who lives in a modest house remarked, "I thought we'd be further along at this point. I feel too old to have such a small house." A man said to me, "I thought when I was thirty, I'd have a better car." Maturity, responsibility, and other attributes that come with growth may mirror endlessly in messages surrounding objects, from the "Big Kid" meals at fast-food restaurants to the taunting message of "still driving/drinking/wearing" something old or inexpensive, and therefore undesirable.

Okay, most of us don't say, "Gee, I guess I ought to feel smaller, less important, and well, left out because I don't own something at this point in my life." But suggestions that it's time to move on with a new object, ensuring that you will belong to a group where you'd like to see yourself abound and where you should be are paired with the tantalizing "could" of a purchase.

❁   ❁   ❁

Of course, ownership can help people feel they belong—for a while at least. Having a beaded headband if you're ten years old may make you feel as much a member of the right group as the diamond solitaire does for the woman twenty years her senior. Possessions offer something for people to have in common: Owning the same sort of house or appliances or car or clothing as your friends makes a difference in how you're perceived—and perhaps, how you perceive your place in the world. But how much does it impact on actually belonging?

Many Envies

"No lawful means can carry me/Out of envy's reach . . ." says Shylock in *The Merchant of Venice*, which Shakespeare wrote around four hundred years ago. So does it still work that way? The word envy comes from both the Old French word *envier*, to desire, and the Latin *invidia,* meaning malice or ill will. To envy someone, along with being an old-time, big-time sin, is about as far from a feeling of belonging as one can get. And I'd argue that the reach of envy—the nose-pressed-up-against-the-glass message of viewing something you want desperately and don't yet have—seems to have lengthened these days.

The material answer to envy, of course, is that you too can buy what you want. How has the roar of the green-eyed monster grown in recent years? Many ways:

Ancestor envy.   The expectation of upward mobility—the idea that surely you will have a better life than your parents or grandparents did—is a long-standing American tradition. But the sense that we're worse off than ever gives way to envy focused on material myth: Everything was more affordable in the past, both parents didn't have to work just to get by, and you deserve to reproduce those circumstances exactly—along with getting the benefits of living in the present, such as antibiotics, jet travel, seeing world events via television, and so on. The notion of, say, inflation or making choices and/or sacrifices takes a holiday.

The number of Americans who say they are "very happy" has declined steadily since the end of World War II. Perhaps it's just people being more forthcoming with their feelings now. But it may play into ancestor/parental envy, which appears to have hit whiny new lows in recent years. Take the recent *New York* magazine article entitled "What It Really Costs to Live in New York," where a marketing executive, making $200,000 a year says, "My mom and dad had a very nice life. Finding an apartment was easier. A house in the country was $25,000. To live that life now, I think you need at least half a million dollars a year." Never mind the possibility that spending $25,000 for a house in the country, in terms of his parents' income, may have been an enormous investment.

Then again, perhaps he's right about the comparative economics. But more important, is it possible that he's overlooking that a "very nice life" can take many different forms?

Ease envy.   Finding an affordable apartment or country house may or may not have been easier in the past. But guess what? According to external wisdom, it's *still* easier for someone else now. In fact, everything is easier for other people, or so it would seem.

Is your life really more difficult than other people's, or does it just feel that way? In the current climate, we usually hear that the answer is the former. Other people aren't as stressed out as you. Other people have the time/money/energy to wear crisp white frocks, pick flowers, and take cooking and home décor seriously. Or play golf without feeling guilty about the kids at home. Or buy the Jaguar they want. Other people are simply more together than you are.

What's their secret? Of course there's always something to buy to free up time, simplify processes, add more energy, add *ease*. Or so we hear.

Aesthetic envy.   "Don't hate me because I'm beautiful," says the slightly vacant model in a magazine. Did you even consider hating her before she told you not to? Does her airbrushed visage have any impact on your life? Well, no. Except that when the challenge is issued, it might make you start thinking. And you might rise to the bait.

The term *shadenfreude* means "harm joy" or taking delight in other people's misery. While viewing other people's good looks doesn't necessarily inspire us to hurl ill will their way, we receive an awful lot of messages identifying a key, a secret to their success which eludes us.

So—do you want to be a model, or just look like one? Aesthetic envy, like ease envy, is based on the ongoing lie of material competition in our culture: Any woman can look just like the airbrushed model in the ad; anyone can craft a stunning découpage with simple materials; anyone can be one of the Beautiful People with Beautiful Lives through buying things. The view that beauty is something that can be photocopied onto any canvas—and be just as good as the original—is rampant. (What else explains why we now see suburban tract mansions that reproduce antebellum Tara on lots so small that, to paraphrase Mark Twain, you could hear your neighbor change her mind?)

The message of accessibility of aesthetics—that your Tara will be *the* Tara, even if it has no cotton fields or trees, that beauty is always a consumer product, and that if someone else has the exact aesthetic that you want, you *can* possess it exactly—may be something we see and hear more frequently.

Provider envy. In the ad, the little girl wants an elephant. Her dad, of course, wants to give it to her. With the magic of modern commercial-making, we see the little girl getting a real baby elephant, walking along euphorically. Since elephants are kind of hard to come by, in the next shot we see another kind of magic happen, this time with a credit card: The little girl, no less euphoric, has a large toy elephant in its stead. Dad's a hero. The fantasy came true.

Isn't that what any parent wants to do? The ad strikes at something real: Your child thinks you've hung the moon, and wouldn't it be great if you could take it down and present it to her? Sure, we don't really believe that anyone would confuse a living elephant with an expensive toy, but the desire to provide is powerful. And the images of what you *can* provide with a purchase are unlimited.

During a bad time a few years ago, provider envy hit me in a big way. I can't even remember the object that brought up the bad feelings, but memories of the unpleasant thoughts running through my head—*we can't afford it, we're letting our kids down, we're depriving them of something important*—linger.

Since my kids lived to thrive without owning the object in question, the possession wasn't really the point. But the *idea* of the possession grew way out of proportion. As did the harsh sense of powerlessness, being unable (or more realistically, in an era of easy credit, in choosing not to spend the money) to provide it.

Provider envy hits you where you breathe. You might not buy something for yourself, but darn it, you want your kids to have it. You want your beloved to have it. You want to do anything in your power to help them feel they belong, so that they know their place in the world and see it as where they want to be. That deep desire, and promises of belonging through objects that promote provider envy, may overtake awareness of what you *do* provide—that can't be bought.

Relationship envy.   While television relationships aren't what they used to be—*Father Knows Best* is no *Married with Children*, the Beav's dealings with Mom, Dad and Wally don't bear much resemblance to families on *South Park* or *The Simpsons*—the desire to belong in the club of happy families, in-love couples, and other strong, healthy relationships is still a no-brainer. "Dysfunctions 'R' Us" isn't a chain store yet, but it could well be one, given how much we learn about things to buy to transform crummy relationships into something enviable.

When I was a child, my family had dinner with some friends of my parents, an unremarkable evening except for one thing: After the plates were cleared, a screaming fight erupted in the kitchen between the teenage daughter and her father about not having a dishwasher. The mother entered into it too, while my family and some other guests sat in embarrassed silence in the dining room next door. If only they had a dishwasher, went the loud lament, their lives wouldn't be so messed up. Their family would be normal. They could have people come to dinner easily, the way everyone else did.

As a child, the solution seemed so obvious to me: If they just bought the dishwasher, everything would be happy again. Even if it cost a lot, it would be worth it, I thought. Except that it didn't work that way. A few months later, they got the dishwasher. And a few months after that, the parents got a divorce.

Clearly, we know that the "belonging" of having happy relationships amounts to a lot more than having certain objects. But even when you're an adult, it's easy to believe otherwise.

What does envy do? Well, certainly it sharpens hunger and alienates: When you feel that others have what you don't, it doesn't do a lot to enhance your sense of belonging. The danger of envy is that, like the pernicious type of weeds gardeners call "thugs," it can spread quickly. It begins to appear everywhere you look. And it's tough to uproot.

I once heard of a rabbi who believed fighting the urge to envy in contemporary life meant turning back to an old tradition in Judaism and other religions: using empathy to overcome envy. He noted the old Yiddish expression of a *peckel of tsuras*, the pack of troubles that everyone, no matter what they possess, carries on his or her back. While it can be hard to imagine much beyond the image of objects, it may help to look at the person you envy instead. What do they have—along with the lovely house, wonderful kid-safe car, and beauty and ease of some sort—that's less than desirable? And really, would you ever trade your own life, despite its flaws, for what they've got?

Missionaries of Materialism

Several years ago, after staying up half the night with a colicky infant, I left my son with a baby-sitter and ventured out to do some errands, since I wasn't good for much else in my sleep-deprived state. Exhausted but stroller-free, I stumbled around my city neighborhood for a while, doing exciting things like picking up the dry cleaning. But soon, as if sleepwalking, I somehow ended up at the counter of a cosmetics store. Needless to say, buying makeup was not on my "to-do" list that day.

The saleswoman was in front of me faster than you can say "dark circles." In retrospect, I realize that I still had the chance to turn around, head home, and take a nap. Even after she spoke to me, I could have politely walked away. But no. Something kept me standing there, as she peered intently at my tired face and postpartum body and asked rapid-fire questions about my "beauty regime." I didn't have many answers—my entire "beauty regime" at that point consisted of trying to make it into the shower before noon—but I suspect she knew that already. I was a live one.

She started out slow, murmuring things about skin types and blotchy complexions and undereye puffiness and "corrective" makeup. Feebly, I mumbled something about staying up all night with a one-month-old. A true professional, she nodded sympathetically, then went in for the kill, her voice trailing off suggestively: "So many women just let themselves go when they have a baby. . . But then there are the ones who just *glow. . .* What you need is a pick-me-up. . . ."

So—did I want to be one of those depressing frumps, or part of a perky group of pretty, cheery new moms? No doubt she said more, but that was the last thing I remember. You may have guessed the end already: in a blur, I left the store with a ridiculous number of beauty products, few of which I ever used.

Of course, that saleswoman was only doing her job. And frankly, in my fatigued condition at the time, you could have sold me nearly anything that promised a pick-me-up.

Generally, it's fairly easy to avoid overzealous professional salespeople, crusading for a commission. What's harder to counter is the amateurs, people I'll call Missionaries of Materialism. They are the people whose faith in material answers is nearly unshakable. And even if you don't feel envious or believe the messages of belonging through objects yourself, there are the people out there who do, fervently, and who are more than happy to spread the Gospel of Owning.

You've probably met one or two Missionaries of Materialism along the way. With near-religious fervor, Missionaries of Materialism tell you that acquisition is the answer to all questions, that shopping is an art form perfected through practice. Their creed? What you purchase is inextricably tied to a higher state of being, from satisfaction in one's relationships to spiritual awareness to emotional stability. You're the better person for buying something.

And since the Missionaries possess the arrogance of the enlightened, they can be pretty convincing. So the $64,000 question is this: When the messages of the Missionaries intrude on actually connecting—or make you feel that you're somehow missing something—how do you opt out of signing up?

The quick and simple answer is, when it gets to be too much, run as fast as you can. Deliberately saying "so what?" to yourself about others' proselytizing may help. But the problem is that Missionaries of Materialism are everywhere, though they probably don't define themselves that way. Studies show a majority of people believe that they themselves aren't materialistic—but most people they know are.

It's worth assessing how much the idea of objects plays into a sense of belonging with certain people—and how it makes you feel. Does it make you feel inadequate, competitive, or, well, bored? Why? Along with thinking about your own response, it's worth considering the Missionaries' intent. Are they sharing their happiness over, say, finding a product that really works, makes them feel good, and might work for you—or are they trying to prove something powerful about themselves? Are they trying to create an inclusive sense of belonging, or set up a situation that separates you from them? Is their motive related to Groucho Marx's tongue-in-cheek comment that "there's no sweeter sound than the crumbling of your fellow man"?

At first glance, Missionaries appear to be motivated by, well, greed. They want more, they plan to have more, they seem motivated to continue the quest of acquisition no matter how much they already have. And they want you to want more. But maybe they're worth viewing another way. Perhaps that greed is really need, the kind that can't completely be satisfied by objects, no matter how many. It's worth considering that greed may be the language of need—the need to belong themselves, the need to be taken seriously, the need to gain positive attention.

A few years ago, I was invited to a full-moon ceremony to be led by a shaman as a birthday celebration for a friend. Instead of gifts, we were told to bring two ideas: something we wanted to let go of, and something we wanted to take into our lives.

I'll admit I quickly dismissed most of the other guests as Missionaries of Materialism. As it grew dark outside, and the shaman prepared for the ceremony in the manicured backyard, they held comfortable ground on familiar topics: a new lawn mower, the handbag someone had just bought, the plans for another bathroom, someone else's good-looking outfit, and a long discussion on home-entertainment systems.

But when we went outside and formed a circle around a small fire, the *terra firma* of the Missionaries got a bit shaky. A couple of people muttered about mosquitoes or grinned in embarrassment, making it clear they were attending this strange event only out of a sense of obligation for their kind but slightly kooky friend and/or their spouses. When the shaman handed us drums to beat, you could almost feel the sullen, irritated thoughts spreading around the circle: This was unfamiliar. This was, well, weird.

One by one, nearly all the faces around the flickering fire closed and hardened, appearing in the darkness like so many stone gargoyles. The shaman tossed herbs into the fire and chanted prayers. The drums, almost grudgingly, it seemed, kept beating.

The shaman chanted more prayers, things about the Earth and elements. The fire and smoke rose into the summer night. The rhythmic beating continued. The shaman chanted and walked around the circle, offering individual blessings.

It was darker out now, and the fire looked bigger and brighter. The pounding of the drums seemed to intensify. The mosquitoes were forgotten, driven elsewhere by the smoke of the fire. And something slowly happened. In the sound of the beating drums and the soothing voice of the shaman giving thanks, in the circle where we stood, the faces of hard-set stone seemed to soften, open.

Led by the shaman, each of us approached the fire with a handful of herbs to symbolize what we wanted to abandon, and tossed it in. And let the smoke hover and swirl for a moment as we thought about what we wanted to take in to our lives.

As each person moved to the center, the circle seemed to expand and contract, strengthen and grow. Without knowing what each person wanted, and without explanation, the experience created a sense of, well, belonging.

It's not every day that you get to beat drums in the moonlight with a bunch of people you might ordinarily write off as hopelessly superficial. On the other hand, the experience made me begin to think that the power to put a person in a different context is always there. The ability to really "belong" may require stepping past the material—to find a place to meet that matters more.

Community and "Consumity"

In recent years, "community" has gotten a bit canonized. In this setup, wistful reminiscence of amicable evenings spent chatting with neighbors on the stoop or front porch, real or imagined, competes with the blue glow of individual television sets (where, perhaps, those porches and stoops come to life as they never did in reality) across the land. The mythology of community, comprised of block parties without disagreements, neighborliness without obligation, and a common cause with nary a dissenting voice, is deeply rooted in American culture. And its so-called demise has given rise to more messages than ever on "consumity," which instantly offers a bit of that belonging through buying.

Like utopian communities of old, suburban real estate listings now promise "real" and "friendly" neighborhoods, "strong," "welcoming," and "family-oriented" blocks along with "privacy" as property values. With an upbeat, frontier-style spirit, houses in new subdivisions are billed as "new communities," part of a larger, like-minded whole, but ready for your own customization. The pull of community, or at least the idea of it in physical space, clearly resonates these days.

But while that pull of community is strong, individual rights, as expressed through private property, may be pushing back harder than ever. According to the American Fence Association, the last decade has seen large, annual increases in the number of fences built. And in recent years, the number of lawsuits surrounding home ownership and property have dramatically increased. As reported in the *New York Times*, a big issue these days isn't just your own backyard, but your neighbors' taste: Disputes and legal action over ugly shutter colors and the aesthetics of jungle gyms are increasingly common.

From the outside, these disputes sound a bit like the defense of Dr. Seuss's Yertle the Turtle, who climbs upon the backs of other, smaller turtles to proclaim himself king "of all that I see." Why can't we all just get along? Of course, there are always two points of view. Debates over your kid's right to play on anything you choose to have in your backyard—as opposed to your neighbor's demand for a view of a nice, open green lawn on your property—can get pretty heated. And you're entitled to your belief that the puce shutters and purple paint are just the thing to pull your house together, even if your neighbors don't like it.

But then, on the other side, maybe the view of your neighbor's laundry and new seven-foot satellite dish didn't figure into the equation when you put all that money down on what you thought would be your dream house. Maybe the new copper roof across the street glares like a mirror in your eyes every time you pull out of the driveway. And maybe the ramshackle, hot-pink house next door seemed charmingly eccentric—until you try to sell your own.

To make matters simpler, many places adopt aesthetic guidelines so that community can just get on with it. When people agree on rules regarding externals, does a greater sense of community reign? As Andrew Ross notes in *The Celebration Chronicles*, an account of living for a year in Disney's planned community of Celebration, Florida, results may be mixed. "No one questioned the goal behind 'being involved,' but for the most part, residents agreed that 'community' had to be earned, not purchased, for it to be real," he writes.

So what "earns" community? Real life isn't an endless film loop of tolerance, acceptance and participation among people who think just as you do, despite advertisements that portray "community" in that way, of course. Still, it's worth weighing the value of compromise between individual wants and building something with others. The current environment of "consumity" presents belonging to a community as a simple process of buying and moving in, and obviously, it hits a lot more than housing. It's up to individuals to decide what makes for real "belonging." But in an environment that constantly touts possessions as a means to that end, it also means deciding, as an individual, what doesn't.

Lifestyle versus Life

"I love my lifestyle but hate my life," someone once remarked to me. Get over it, you might say. Get a life.

We might not have believed Robin Leach's hokey pitch about "champagne wishes and caviar dreams" when he glowed over a celebrity's gold-plated bathroom fixtures in *Lifestyles of the Rich and Famous*, but we watched his "reality-based" television show anyway. And if we didn't exactly buy into the babble, we listened. In recent years, having a lifestyle—the "integrated way of life of an individual as typified by his manner, attitudes, possessions, etc." according to *Webster's* dictionary—has moved from low-budget TV to media outlets everywhere. And it's emerged as a reasonable facsimile for living.

While a "lifestyle" itself appears as ever-optimistic, light-hearted, and desirable, the objects you need to maintain it are presented as superserious business. Yes, you're spending something, and those decisions matter. But when you factor in "lifestyle," the solemnity surrounding ownership choices gains a special kind of gravity: It's not just kitchen cabinets or what you buy at the liquor store or where you do your grocery shopping, it's your *way of life!*

The serious pursuit of having a lifestyle may affect how we feel about life. More than fifty years ago, in his essay "My Wood," E. M. Forster reflected that acquiring a piece of land made him feel heavy, weighed down: "The Gospels. . . point out what is perfectly obvious, yet seldom realized: If you have a lot of things you cannot move about a lot, that furniture requires dusting, dusters require servants, servants require insurance stamps, and the whole tangle of them makes you think twice before you accept an invitation to dinner or go for a bathe in the Jordan."

Do objects make you beg off about going to dinner or taking a splash in any river of your choosing, causing you to miss an experience with other people because too much time winds up belonging to belongings? Let's say you manage to accept the invitation anyway, leaving the object—the wood, in Forster's case—at home. Despite your best efforts at levity, the weight of possessions may come along, uninvited—and end up dominating the gathering.

With your possessions come those of other people to weigh things down as well. Where are the jokes, the great stories, the debates over politics or philosophies or anything else that gives life to a social gathering? Consumption may be the universal language in our culture, but how does it affect sharing ideas? Or having a laugh? Crushed by the seriousness of comparative values and comparison shopping, dominated by the solidity and stolidity of *things*, fun may beat a hasty retreat.

Of course, the enjoyment we get from certain objects balances the time and energy that they may consume; sure, it's a bore to polish the wood floor, but it looks awfully nice when it's done. Living in the material world naturally requires acquisition, attention, and upkeep of possessions; the question is, how heavily does it weigh on spontaneity, humor, and fun in one's life? What does it do to interaction that helps us feel we "belong"?

As Forster points out, the responsibility inherent in ownership of objects may be "obvious." When the image of lifestyle neglects to include the nuances of real life, things can get pretty ugly. The vacation home pictured in the real estate ad features photos of picnics by the lake, not the pipes bursting in the winter when you're not there. The spilled red wine becomes a full-fledged disaster when it involves the silk-covered couch you haven't yet finished paying for.

Lifestyle can get pretty darned demanding. Despite Forster's feeling "heavy" from owning his wood, he also finds that "it makes me feel that it ought to be larger," and that he "ought to do something to it." A woman I spoke with liked her new Jeep—but after owning it for a year, felt she needed a "dressier" car to use at night. Does anticipation and expectation get in the way of enjoying what's already there, becoming a burden? When the promise of pleasure recedes with actual ownership, what next?

Since there's a lot of seriousness linked to objects these days, it's worth lightening up a bit and thinking about what belonging really means. It's worth considering the lyrics of the song "The Good Ship Lifestyle," by the band Chumbawumba. The narrator in the song tells how his friends have abandoned the fictional boat. Since he's the only one left on it, he's elected himself captain of the "Good Ship Lifestyle," which might be fine, except for one thing. As he puts it, "This is the loneliest voyage I've ever been on. . . ."

And here's an idea that sounds nearly radical in the current climate: Forget objects and style—what improves your *life*?

6

⌣∶∽

LOVE

In Margery Williams's 1922 children's story, *The Velveteen Rabbit,* an old, worn toy horse tells a new stuffed rabbit, "When a child loves you for a long, long time, not just to play with, but REALLY loves you, then you become Real." The details are, uh, fuzzy, but the horse assures the little rabbit that he became a real horse years ago, even if he looks a bit decrepit in the nursery. But somewhere else, he's a living creature. As for becoming real, he says, "It doesn't happen all at once. . . You become. It takes a long time. . . ."

In this old-fashioned tale, the toy eventually *does* become a real rabbit because a little boy loves him. At the story's end, he's frolicking in a field somewhere, even when his stuffed self is discarded. The book's appeal has probably lasted because the allegory rings true: Love *can* transform people, if not stuffed animals. It takes time and patience. And real love doesn't depend on, say, a shiny coat or bright button eyes, but feeling.

Ah, the power of love! The old story of the velveteen rabbit—love animating the inanimate—is the inverse of so many
messages these days regarding love and objects. If you listen to
external wisdom, you generally don't hear about love giving
life, but about objects keeping love alive. You don't hear about
the process of simply slogging through what love sometimes requires, but about infusions of love via a stream of stuff. And
love itself—"real" feeling—isn't enough. Instead, love is real
when it's an object. And the object is a direct reflection of the
quantity and quality of feeling.

We've long had tokens of love, as well as charms and potions
to create and keep it. Take wedding bands. Ancient Egyptians
believed that a "vein of love" ran from the fourth finger of the
left hand to the heart; ancient Romans were the first to use an
unbroken circle of metal on this finger to represent the marriage contract. By the 1100s, Pope Innocent the Third decreed
that church-wedding ceremonies had to include a ring.

Which brings us to the diamond engagement ring. In 1477,
Maximillian of Austria never had to hear that "two months'
salary is about right" to spend on something to woo Mary of
Burgundy, but allegedly, someone important advised him to
buy her a diamond, which she accepted, along with his marriage proposal. This event—giving a gift of a rare, sparkling,
and durable substance signifying purity, harmony, passion, and
other magical properties—supposedly kicked off the tradition
that continues today. Regardless of karats or carats, the symbolic value of these things endures.

The breadth of love tokens has expanded in recent years,
and the message that feeling is inextricably fused with objects

is louder than ever. How do we learn that one can't exist without the other? Count the ways:

The "commoditization" of feeling.   Love—romantic or familial, immeasurable and powerful—is now presented as, well, a commodity. Purchasing an object isn't positioned as just a demonstration of love, it's loving itself.

As a commodity, nearly anything qualifies as love, according to external wisdom. For years, we've heard from a cake-mix maker, "Nothin' says lovin' like somethin' from the oven." We read that canned soup is love. So is the right brand of diapers or dog biscuits. In case you worry whether your child feels cherished while you're away, you can always leave the snack that specifically "tastes like somebody loves you"—as opposed to some old indifferent piece of fruit, for example. And if the rapture, comfort, companionship or any other component of love is elusive in your life, well, you can always "discover the feeling" with a credit card.

You can't actually *buy* love, of course: Anyone who has ever loved knows it's either there or it's not, that it's returned or it isn't. It can't be measured or counted like a commodity. But objects can. And when objects and love become intertwined, it almost seems that love itself can be bought, bartered, or borrowed—for a price.

"Real" caring gets quantified.   We may be fully aware that feeling can't be exchanged for so many dollars, but it doesn't mean we can't try. Not long ago, I heard about a woman who counted the number—and price—of items her mother-in-law

gave to her baby daughter. She kept a running tally, too, of the items her sister-in-law received for her son. No matter what this woman received, she perceived favoritism, with her own child as loser. Did fewer or cheaper objects demonstrate a lack of love, or did she imagine it? Was it worth comparing the amount and quality of love for each grandchild as materialized in baby clothes and toys, as opposed to simply accepting what her child received?

It's possible that the mother-in-law was impossible, that she didn't much care for the daughter-in-law or her child, and that she did play shameless favorites that took shape with objects. It hurts to feel that you or your child is less cherished than others.

On the other hand, to paraphrase Eleanor Roosevelt, someone can make you feel inferior only with your consent. The pop-cultural yardstick of objects to measure affection is one that may get whipped out incessantly. So here's the point: *In your own life, it doesn't have to.*

Since most of us are too busy to take umbrage over baby clothes, or to expend energy wondering whether the price of a rattle or wedding entertainment reflects loving feeling or not, the daisy-plucking "loves me, loves me not" may not come up very often with objects. But given the countless ways in our culture to "count the ways" with material things, uncertainty over how someone feels about you, as expressed through stuff, may hover in the background.

But what's in it for me?   A recently single man told me, "The only thing that women care about is the kind of car you drive and how much money you make." Oh, puhleeze, I thought.

Tempted to deliver a tart reply, it suddenly occurred to me that he might have a good point: about himself and perhaps his environment. He cared deeply about his car, so he assumed all women would, too. He wasn't meeting anyone he liked, and he didn't have a fancy car. Therefore, it must be his lack of something material—as opposed to his less-than-admirable ability to listen or his propensity to make sweeping generalizations about an entire gender—that was to blame for his lousy love life.

When attracting love is positioned as something that can be bought or sold, getting what you want seems pretty simple. As a result, the concept of manipulation—with objects and through other means—may gain attention, if not validity. Like the logic that guy applied, here, love isn't the end, something magical and real that exists between two people. It's ownership that gets you what *you* want.

Whether that goal is an attractive mate who listens attentively and adoringly or a child that makes you proud, objects of love may get aligned with a desired outcome. Never mind that real love may be a give and take, and that most people can't be manipulated and trained like seals responding to a bucket of fish. Regardless of the logo on the bucket.

The idea that extrinsic change through objects will somehow bring about intrinsic transformation in another person—to just how you want them to be—has spread from the realm of advertising to emerge as an editorial staple: variations of "How to Make Him/Her Do Whatever You Want" appeared on no fewer than eight magazine covers one recent month. Desired results, they claim, may be as close as a gift or a good meal.

Guilt springs eternal.   Part of manipulation is guilt, always a sharp motivator. And it's more finely honed than ever in our materialism-driven culture. Based on the notion of achievable perfection, the guilt-machine goes full blast, stoking a furnace of bad feelings. Are you depriving your children, neglecting your spouse, or letting down your parents? Of course you are! We all do sometimes. But now you can get out of bad feelings by buying something!

Of course, guilt-provoking messages we receive may feed upon something that's already there. Rationally, we're aware that there are no perfect relationships, that nobody is a model parent, child, or spouse all the time. But then, we can always find a way to feel remiss in some way. And that's where objects may push in as a solution.

Those solutions spring eternal. The problem, of course, is that the guilty feelings may be ever-replenishing as well, regardless of things we buy ourselves or gifts we give to others to assuage them. So instead, perhaps it's worth considering some ways to cultivate "innocence," not through buying, but through doing.

Sex, love and videotape.   The promise of sex sells stuff, with or without love thrown in. Although the triad of sex, wealth, and power has always been a magnet of desire, it's difficult to imagine when great sex was ever so constantly celebrated as something that could be, well, acquired. For better or worse, sex has moved from back-room magazine and video racks to the mainstream in recent years. Consumers of all ages now receive countless media messages and images—a veritable *Kama Sutra* of consumption on the subject!—about desiring it, getting it, improving it. And never has the promise of intimacy through sex been so clearly articulated as a promise of love.

But only if you're worthy of it. What's sexy? Of course it's in the eye—and mind, heart and body—of the beholder. Given the current, near-obsessional focus on obtaining sexual intimacy, however, it's limited to a lucky few.

Sure, you may be in good shape, but how's your "sexual fitness"? You may look okay in clothes, but how will you feel about your naked self during a sexual encounter? Not up on the latest look, tricks, or attire to enhance sexuality? There's always something to purchase to ensure you'll snare someone's attention—and guarantee peak performance. While sex isn't love, the messages we receive equate the promise of being beloved with having the right "equipment"—and the possibility of lonely lovelessness without it.

"Let not to the marriage of true minds admit impediments," wrote Shakespeare, no slouch on the subject of love. These days, more "impediments"—the meaning ascribed to objects, the feeling in relationships promised with a purchase—may push at the gates of authentic love harder than ever. We can't do much about the battering ram of those messages. But we can disengage from the onslaught to develop alternatives. We can work to extricate objects from affection, to give and receive love that is unconditional. And we can work on building the kind of love that Shakespeare described as an "ever-fixed mark" that "alters not," independent of worldly goods or what the world might toss us.

Marriage, Money, and Stuff

He's cheap, and she just loves to shop. She's a worrywart about their savings account, and he just wants to have a good time. She thinks he's spoiling the kid with the expensive baseball mitt; he sees it as a necessity. Or he thinks she's spoiling the kid with new party shoes, and she sees them as a necessity. He wants the sports car, she wants the new kitchen. Do any of these stories sound familiar?

Or how about this one: He gives her a toaster when what she really wanted was lingerie. Or he gives her lingerie, when what she really wanted was the toaster.

Can these marriages be saved? Add a laugh track and these scenarios sound like the basis for a sitcom, where, of course, the problem will get resolved by the end of the show. (Hey, why not buy both the toaster and the lingerie?) But they reflect something that might strike a nerve in real life.

Love may be all you need, but, as the old saying goes, you can't live on it. Money might not be the most important thing in your relationship, but studies show that differences of opinion between partners on how to spend it is a top problem in marriages.

A loaf of bread, a jug of wine and thou may be well and good in the pages of poetry, but forging a life together involves lots of other objects as well. While the expression "tying the knot" may have come from an ancient ceremony of binding two people with rushes to symbolize their spiritual and emotional union, it also indicated that marriage was, and continues to be, a binding financial transaction—a joining of both people and property. Although a bride's dowry that specified so many sheep or salvers in exchange for the groom's love, honor and protection may be a thing of the past, those roots remain. And, between prenuptial agreements and increasingly intricate divorce laws, it's become more complex in recent years.

Certainly, part of the pleasure of building a partnership and family lies in creating a home for shared feelings and shared property. This is where expectations of objects may come in, and where individual connections to the idea of "things" may clash with truly feeling connected with another person.

Images of the stages of happy marriages coupled with ownership appear all over: the blissful newlyweds in their apartment, the "starter house," and maybe a baby. A few years later, there's another baby, a bigger home, and a neighborhood with good schools. Follow the perfect couple through the archetypes of acquisition and the things just keep getting bigger and better: the fur coat or sports car for the big birthday, the state-of-the-art media room for wholesome family-time together, something set in platinum. . . . We may not believe that marital love is made manifest through more possessions, but external wisdom presents it as the way it is.

The images of happy unity through property run in tandem with equal, if not greater numbers of messages on self-fulfillment through stuff, which may pose a constant, potential conflict. Even if you don't pay attention to most of the hype, it's out there. When you constantly get the message that objects are the answer to finding yourself, they may intrude on having what you want with someone else.

"Along with air, earth, water, and fire, money is the fifth nat-ural force a human being has to reckon with most often," wrote the poet and essayist Joseph Brodsky. Like the other elements, it's necessary for survival. And it's a powerful metaphor.

Pick a metaphor, any metaphor: Little comes close to the multiple meanings that money takes on in our culture. Not un-like tasteless tofu, it absorbs what surrounds it: good or evil, lib-eration or a burden, selfishness or selflessness, caring or con-trolling. The power of money is that the same, neutral dollar—or a thousand—can take on so many different flavors.

This power can get magnified when it comes to objects. Take that thousand dollars and turn it into wide screen TV. Translate it into a treadmill or a couple of killer outfits. And if you don't happen to have the money, charge it. The personal meaning of the TV, the treadmill, or the clothes for the person who buys them may not have any bearing on the relationship, but then again, it might.

For one person an object may signify "fun"; for another, it spells "selfish." A "necessity" for one member of a couple may be "frippery" to the other. Fights about "not enough" money may be the aftermath of a shared, what-the-heck shopping spree or simply paying the bills. But they're often generated by differing ideas of what's "essential." And the problem snowballs when individual expectations of "must-have" objects over-whelm commitment to something more important with an-other person.

Since we live in an environment that exults in images of "av-erage" happy couples cooking together at $6,000 ranges, the message of having a better relationship through having better things may be louder than ever. And since we're also subject to the message of shopping as self-affirmation that's *good* for us, force-fed the urge to splurge—and the heck with anyone else—it may enter into our relationships.

Anyone can probably think of an object—or idea of an object—that may have prompted strong feelings in their relationships. What were those feelings? What was the impact on the relationship?

Take the '66 Mustang that a man I know had. He'd bought it for next to nothing, lovingly refurbished it himself, and ended up, after five long years of working on it, with a beautiful classic car. During that time, he'd gotten married and had two children. The car still demanded his time, and his wife, who had once encouraged his hobby, began to resent the demands that she believed the car made on their lives. As she put it, "It was too valuable and delicate to use very often, and my husband was the only one who knew just how to make it run. I started joking that the car was like 'Christine,' the possessed vehicle in Stephen King's novel. Except that it stopped being funny at a certain point. I actually started hating the car, feeling jealous of it. Even though he knew the car no longer fit into our lives, it was very hard for my husband to decide to sell it. But our relationship definitely improved when he finally got rid of it."

It took a lot for her husband to reassess how the car—that he'd worked on so long and had once enjoyed so much—now contributed to his life. And in the end, he says he's glad he gave it up. So perhaps combating the power that objects may wield in a loving relationship involves considering values—not the ones in catalogues, but those you hold together. What do you want most in your relationship—forget objects—that's not there? What good things exist in the relationship that faith in possessions may be obscuring?

And it's possible that extricating your own feelings from possessions—and perhaps, trying to understand your partner's—is a place to start. A woman I spoke with was furious that her husband was angry she had bought a big-ticket item—with money she had earned—without discussing it with him first. Though they could well afford it, it's telling that he focused on the expense instead of the communication rift.

So what did money—and the object—mean here? Control versus mutual respect? Acknowledgment versus ignoring? Needs not getting met? Who knows? But what each brought to the item, obviously, came between them. For that couple, as well as the rest of us, it might be worth thinking about common goals—and how far ownership goes to further them.

Given the amount of time we spend shopping, free time may have a way of turning into a sprint of errands surrounding stuff: running from one store to the next, maintaining property, acquiring more. And given the energy that objects demand, it may be difficult to find the time to cultivate experience or discuss what really matters.

It's worth taking a break from the bills, the shopping, and the fixing, and schedule time for a nonmaterial activity. One woman who tried this told me, "It doesn't have to be a big getaway. We just took a walk together and talked. And it helped." The point is that spending time purchasing and connecting to stuff may take a backseat to connecting to the person you love. What's your priority?

The Best Gifts

"It's the thought that counts," we tell ourselves and our children. And while we'd like to assume those thoughts are all loving and good, gifts may convey other meanings: hostility, disappointment, manipulation, overbearing control, to name a few. The power of gifts to communicate may not make or break a relationship, but they may become a symbol for what's there—or what isn't.

That power in objects may live on: What gifts communicate in thought can last far longer than the gift itself. One woman recalled that her slender mother frequently criticized her weight—and then gave her size "petite" sweaters, far too small for her to ever wear. "The thought always came through loud and clear," she says, "that I was too big. I knew she loved me in other ways. But those sweaters always made me feel awful."

But maybe it's all in the eye of the beholder. Another woman said that she, too, received a too-small sweater for her birthday from her fiancé, and "I loved it. That little sweater made me believe he saw me as skinnier than I really was."

The worst presents—those the French call *cadeaux empoissonés*, or "poison gifts"—may be memorable because they tell us who we should be, without acknowledging who we are. You can probably think of one poison gift—the unasked-for gift of the gerbil for the teacher, or the drum set for the child of overworked, sleep-deprived parents. Even worse, they might tell us how we've failed, without accepting our success.

But not all are ill-intentioned, as novelist Milan Kundera explores in his novel *Immortality*, through the complicated, difficult character Laura, who gives a piano to her sister. "Laura beamed: 'I wanted to give you something that will force you to think of me even when I'm not with you.'. . . When she bought her sister the piano it was mainly because she wanted to teach her niece how to play. Brigitte, however, hated the piano. . . And so the whole affair ended badly, and after a few months the piano was reduced to a mere show object, or rather a nuisance object; to a sad reminder of failure. . . that nobody wanted."

Especially if you're receiving it, you know right away what makes a gift malicious or manipulative, and how painfully possessions can communicate these qualities. But what do good gifts have in common? I got some surprising answers.

Contrary to the myriad messages we receive that link expense with desirability, it seems that price had little to do with "best" among the many people I asked. One man said his best gift was a red electric guitar he received for his bar mitzvah. A woman said, without hesitation, that her all-time best gift was a purple, fringed leather purse. Another mentioned a jar of jam she received years ago.

Why? "My parents had always encouraged me to play classical piano. Even though I desperately wanted a guitar to play rock and roll, it wasn't something they wanted me to do," said the man who received the guitar. "When they gave me a guitar the day I 'became a man' the gesture spoke to me. My parents acknowledged what *I* wanted to be and become."

The woman who mentioned the purple purse said, "When I was a teenager, I was in a store with my aunt and the rest of my family, and saw a fringed, purple suede bag that I couldn't stop admiring. I knew I'd get a lecture about how ungrateful and frivolous I was for even wanting such a thing if I asked for it. My aunt must have seen me, because later that day, she gave me the bag. I don't think I've ever been so happy or surprised to get something."

"When my parents were going through an ugly divorce," says the woman who cited the jam, "my brother and I would hide in my room and eat jam and bread when they fought. It was sort of a ritual for us, and it made me feel better. Years later, when I went to college, I was very nervous. And when I got there and opened my trunk I found a jar of the jam my brother put there. It was the best gift I ever got, because it made me believe he believed in me, that he would be there for me if things got bad, but mostly, that things were going to be okay."

One of my own "best gifts" came to me when I was eleven years old: a fluorescent green miniskirt and vest set, made from some polyester fabric that smelled terrible and looked suspiciously flammable. In retrospect, I understand that it was, in a word, hideous. But at the time, hanging in the department store, it spoke to a gawky, bespectacled preteen.

Certainly, it didn't appeal much to my mother, who, reasonably enough, thought it was ugly and badly made, to boot. But she put her own opinions and desires aside and tried to understand what I saw in the skirt and vest, worked to see them as I did. And, standing in the overlit store, she suddenly got it: Despite her own feelings, she recognized me and what I wanted. Needless to say, I got skirt and vest, and wore them until they turned gray.

Another best gift from my own life arrived many years later, under very different circumstances. I had a job I hated, and was trying to write and get published in my off hours in the hopes of forging a different career. So far, I'd gotten a couple of rejections, and my confidence was a bit shaky. But finally, amazingly, a small chain of newspapers decided to run a weekly column I proposed. Suddenly, I had a byline. I was, gulp, a freelance writer, getting paid a princely sum of thirty-five dollars a week for the privilege.

Well, sort of. I couldn't exactly quit my day job with those earnings. But it was a start.

Around that time, my husband came home with a book he'd picked up for me. It was a reference guide for freelance writers. Sure, it was something I could have picked up myself, or used in the library. But the fact that he thought to give it to me spoke volumes: Support, validation, and encouragement of what I really wanted to be and do.

The skirt set is long-gone and the book is now out of date. No doubt the guitar has been traded in, the purple purse lost, and the jam eaten. What remains are the thoughts behind the gifts, the enduring value of unconditional love from another person.

A gift can't take the place of loving, but it may say something. What's the best gift you've ever received? What did it tell you about your relationship with the giver? What did it affirm in yourself? What did you once give to someone else that really mattered to them?

Interestingly, people I asked about the best gifts they had ever received found it more difficult to come up with the best gift they'd ever given to someone else. It's harder to know how someone else has felt, certainly, than how you've felt yourself. So perhaps it's something to consider when deciding on a gift: What does that person want, not just in an object, but on a deeper level? What have they communicated to you about themselves—how they'd like to see themselves, their hopes or dreams—that you can validate not only in the objects you give, but with the kindness of your intent?

Letting Go

The best gifts involve giving up preconceived "shoulds"—abandoning the idea of what the person you love should do or be, as demonstrated through objects. And perhaps having what we want in relationships with other people involves decisions about what we need to give up in our own relationships with things.

It's not just about rethinking "love me, love my car too" or "you don't love my car, so you won't love me." It's about taking a hard look at where connections to objects may get in the way of *acting* to have what we want most.

I heard about a man who got very angry with his seven-year-old one Saturday because she had knocked over a framed poster that had been sitting in their basement for a long time. The man had felt overworked and grumpy, and without thinking, he said, he blew up at his daughter. "I started screaming about having respect for other people's things and being careless. I knew it was an accident, but I lost it."

What was supposed to be time they'd spend together that weekend had turned into a torrent of tears and shouts. "I was cleaning up the broken glass, and my daughter was in her room crying when I suddenly saw the poster for what it was. I'd spent all week looking forward to spending time with my daughter. And I was ruining it by screaming about a piece of paper I didn't even like much."

The man apologized, and said the incident made him start thinking about what he really wanted in his relationship with his daughter. "I was putting the 'thing' ahead of her, and I had to let go of that. I was equating respect for me with respect for a poster. I needed to look at what really happened, and how my reaction could hurt the relationship I want to have with my daughter. I had to give up that kind of thinking to get what I want."

Parenting experts have said that it's not what you say as a parent that counts, it's who you are. It's not even what you do, as much as how you approach things. The cultural influences that link objects with a higher power, of course, affect our kids. But they may also affect us, and what we teach our kids as well. What values do we want to pass on? How do our own relationships with objects speak as loudly as what we teach?

There's the evergreen story about the small child who gets the expensive birthday present: To the parents' dismay, the big box it comes in is much more entertaining than the toy itself. The child spends her birthday climbing in and out of the box, putting it on her head, making people laugh. It might be worth considering that box—so simple and plain—when thinking about love and objects.

And perhaps that means retrieving conditions—or meaning—that we ascribe to *objects* in a relationship to have what we want in the relationship itself. It's not easy. As any parent knows, sitting down with a three-year-old and playing for two hours with a box requires more of yourself than handing the kid yet another new toy. It requires more energy to work with an eight-year-old on understanding math than it does to use an object to bribe him to achieve desired results on a test. Or to take the time to discuss things that matter more in life than the message that "more is better" that kids hear constantly.

It may extend to other loving relationships as well. Commitment to another person may involve committing to a shared checking account, but demonstrating acceptance and respect—and committing to cultivating love—means a lot more. We are constantly inundated with messages identifying what could be with another purchase. But how can you work with what's there—now?

Cutting attachments to the idea of objects—as love, self-fulfillment, or anything else—requires coming up with alternatives. Dematerializing love may mean discussing dreams and ideas of what you value and how you both want to live together, not simply what you want to buy together or separately—not giving and getting gifts. It may involve accepting that you and your partner have different expectations of objects—and working together to come to a compromise. And it may mean acting selflessly sometimes to build the relationship as opposed to being right—or building oneself up.

Our cultural focus is so often on what's wrong or what could be improved. So here's the flip side: What qualities does your partner, parent, or child possess that are enough, or more than enough? Working to acknowledge, on a daily basis, something that's special, unique, and good in the people you love—to them and to yourself—may be a way to find more satisfaction in those relationships. Which goes beyond what one can buy.

7

⤸⟐⤹

DOING THE RIGHT THING

The fruit of the righteous is a tree of life.

—PROVERBS 11:30

You can almost hear the grandfatherly twinkle of an eye in the voice-over that reassures us, "It's the right thing to do." He's not talking about telling the truth, doing something difficult but necessary, or taking a stand against something wrong. The warm, husky voice is telling us about breakfast cereal. And the message here—as with so many purchasable solutions—is that somehow, buying and consuming the right morning meal is a virtue in and of itself.

Whether you're talking about young people, business professionals, or politicians, the subject of the "decline in morals" in society has come up since people put stylus to clay tablets, and it still marches on. Whether people are truly less ethical than ever remains open for debate, but one thing is certain: At heart, nearly nobody wants to believe that they are unethical, wrong, amoral. Nearly anyone, regardless of cultural, economic, racial, and religious differences, wants to believe they're morally grounded, with a firm grasp of what's right and what's not, and will act in good conscience when tested.

Of course, actually doing the right thing—or even knowing for sure what that "right thing" may be—isn't always so simple. But help is here. While morals may or may not be in decline, moralizing is alive and well, trumpeted from the pulpits of popular culture. With omnipresent messages that objects hold goodness, choosing virtue over vice is as accessible as your wallet.

Now, it's hard to imagine that anyone truly confuses all those thirty-second tidings of great goodness with, say, the Ten Commandments, or believes, for example, that they will become more Gandhi-like because they buy a computer that uses an image of the great leader in its ad campaign. But conscience is a powerful thing, and in the current climate, it's difficult to escape the consciousness, on some level, of good and evil as defined by what you own or consume. It's hard to avoid the message that righteousness is implicit in the act of buying.

The messages of morality through purchasing are especially effective because they're simplistic. Unlike the real "right thing to do," which requires time, thought, and difficult, often painful decision-making, purchasing offers a shortcut to virtue.

Think of the voice-overs in a television ad that are a litany of do-good New Year's resolutions. This year, we hear from the first person, "I'll have more fun." Another chimes in that this year, "I'll spend more time with my family." The last resolution we hear is classic: "I'll save money." The whole time we're listening to these heartfelt pledges, the camera is lingering lovingly on a minivan. Clearly, it's positioned as the answer to not just one, but *all* of these good intentions.

Of course, you can't be "good" all the time. Temptations abound. But unlike the story of Eve, the serpent, and the apple or other morality tales of desire and consequences, we now hear that paradise is perpetually up for sale at cut-rate prices— and with no repercussions.

What's real "temptation"? In the traditional sense, giving in to temptation is doing something you know isn't right. It's self-serving, at the possible expense of harming yourself or another person, or, if you're talking about it on a really big scale, all of mankind. It's a weakness, a lapse in strength of character, a fleeting fulfillment of individual desire that may turn out to be bad news in the end.

Today's "temptation" is less about connections to others than it is about invented fulfillment: Since so many things are positioned as both objects of desire and panaceas to any sort of evil, there's no bad news. If you buy the right thing, we hear, you can even do something "bad" and get away with it. You can have your cake and eat it too, if you buy the right brand. Sure, you may never have considered the morality of polishing off a pint of ice cream, but when it's positioned as something you can do "guilt-free," go for it!

When deciding between the toaster pastry or the bowl of oatmeal, among telephone service providers or brands of computers or anything else that you purchase and consume emerges as an ethical dilemma, how does it affect actually doing the right thing? When products are imbued with morality, when purchasing is aligned with virtue, what happens when you don't buy in? Most important, how do we turn off the roar of moralizing through objects in our culture to hear—and do— the honorable thing ourselves?

Honor and Objects

A student of mine once compared acquisition to religion: "We worship at the altar of the cash register," he wrote. The "god of 'ka-ching!'" as a friend calls this phenomenon, may have no bearing on your own spiritual or ethical framework. But we live in a culture that doesn't just accept, but "honors" credit cards—and meshes personal integrity with a purchase. This may muddle ends and means, and intrude on living by what we know to be right.

The cultural call for "personal responsibility" and "accountability" has gotten louder, or at least has a larger megaphone these days. Impassioned demands for the return of honor and "character" emerges in discussions about everything from education to taxes. It's a fine idea. But the call for these high-minded virtues runs counter to the maelstrom of other messages we receive from various media.

It's complicated. The vast number of half-truths or outright lies we need to question each day—no, you won't turn into a fairy princess if you get the doll, and yes, you still have to pay for the sofa even if it *is* "free for six months"—are part of the background noise of our lives. The immorality (or morality) of debt has shifted from buying "on time" to the more upbeat "getting credit" over the last fifty-odd years, and that attitude is now aided by a massive number of solicitations urging us to get yet another card. Personal responsibility, of course, involves how we respond to these messages: Credit cards don't destroy people's integrity or lives, people do that to themselves. We might file the ethically questionable images of what easy credit and objects can do for us in a mental trash bin, but they may still remain in our heads.

An editorial called "Modern-Day Slavery" published in the *New York Times* in September 2000 asserts that some 20 million people throughout the world live in forced servitude. In a particularly chilling detail, the article notes, "A girl in a northern Thai village can be sold into prostitution for $2,000—a huge sum there. A Thai survey found that many families knowingly sold their daughters into prostitution because they felt pressure to buy consumer goods such as televisions." Sadly, children have always been sold into various kinds of slavery throughout the world, but this example presents an especially devastating new interpretation of "survival"—a television in exchange for a life—and the reach and power of consumer "pressure."

The connection between desire—or pressure—for objects and immorality doesn't get much more extreme. And while we may not end up on the brink of financial ruin, possibly imperiling ourselves or our families for the sake of, say, another car, the example begs a question: What's doing the enslaving here? And how does it affect ethics and personal honor?

Kalle Lasn, the founder of *Adbusters* magazine who writes eloquently and disparagingly about consumer culture in *Culture Jam: The Uncooling of America* advocates battling rampant media messages of desire—and the corporations that produce them—with action. He writes about a "moment of truth" in a supermarket parking lot, when his rage at having to deposit a quarter for the privilege of using a shopping cart overtook him: "A little internal fuse blew. . . I banged that coin in tight until it jammed. I didn't stop to think whether this was ethical or not—I just let my anger flow. . . ." Lasn defends his actions by saying, "Once you realize that consumer capitalism is by its very nature unethical, and therefore, it's unethical *not* to jam it. . . once you start trusting yourself and relating to the world as an empowered human being instead of a hapless consumer drone, something remarkable happens. Your cynicism dissolves."

Ethical or not, consumer capitalism is what we have at the moment. And until someone comes up with some other, perfect solution for all people in a democracy, that's what we'll have for a while. So we'll put the political aside for a moment to consider the personal: In his rage, Lasn neglects to connect his actions to other people. While he makes relevant points, he never bothers to consider the next person in line who needs a cart or the supermarket worker making minimum wage who may have to stand out in the rain for an hour trying to unjam the machine. He overlooks the idea that two wrongs don't make a right.

Or that true ethical empowerment may lie, not in destroying property, but in questioning our own, personal relationships to it. "Hapless consumer drone" or enlightened radical, we're all subject to the same messages. How we choose to react to them, however, has got to come down to our own sense of integrity. And connecting our own actions involving objects to their effect on other people.

Modern-Day Deadly Sins

Literal belief in the demonic guy with the pitchfork may be on the wane these days, but that doesn't mean that a strong sense of sin is absent from a materialism-driven environment. Far from it: Old-style, strict rules on right and wrong—and retribution—still apply when it comes to objects of desire.

But recently, the rules have changed. Sure, the traditional Seven Deadly Sins may have some meaning, but it's the new ones we hear about a lot more now. What's really, *really* bad these days? Forget Pride or Covetousness and consider what I think of as the Modern-Day Deadly Sins:

Vulnerable.   The Sensitive Male as a cultural ideal may have had a brief moment in the sun in the 1970s, but that was before Men from Mars and the World Wrestling Federation. And frankly, even back then, "sensitive" as a virtue had limits, which, when crossed, could put you perilously close to being a wuss. The same holds true today: sensitive may still be okay when it comes to liking puppies, differentiating between thread counts in sheets or, say, taking care of your skin with a state-of-the-art shaving cream. When it crosses into vulnerability, today's man had still better watch out.

Hubris, the old Greek idea of impassioned contempt or arrogance, has come into its own in a materialized environment. With so many material ways to cultivate hubris—from defying the elements to protecting yourself against emotional turmoil—being vulnerable becomes a sin. And while the Golden Rule hasn't yet become "Do unto others before they do unto you," the message is that if something bad happens, it could have been prevented.

Preparation for any eventuality, no matter how unexpected, is always available through objects, according to the wisdom of those seeking to make a sale. The upside of vulnerability—openness that could result in some unanticipated pleasure or newfound wisdom—goes unmentioned. Instead, it's liability, weakness, and disaster waiting to happen.

While we hear that invincibility may be only a purchase away, it's interesting to note that hubris and vulnerability have become increasingly popular entertainment topics in recent years. Best-sellers such as Jon Krakauer's *Into Thin Air* and Sebastian Junger's *The Perfect Storm,* as well as "created reality" television shows like *Survivor* examine where invincibility begins and ends. In Krakauer's account of an ill-fated trip up Mount Everest, no amount of state-of-the-art outerwear, no means of communication, however advanced the modem, and certainly, not even the most absurd material detail—the infamous espresso maker a climber brought—could spare anyone from the elements on the deadly expedition. In *The Perfect Storm*, high winds and huge waves off the coast of Massachusetts prove too much even for highly experienced fishermen, despite their best attempts to survive. And although contestants in *Survivor* are battling for a shot at a million bucks rather than really fighting for their lives, the show's popularity indicates we're fascinated by the testing of the limits of hubris—and witnessing others' vulnerability.

To find there are elements that can't be conquered—or to accept the concept that some events can't be controlled by the right equipment and knowledge—is anathema to materialism-driven values. Is it possible that these stories are especially popular now because they compellingly remind us that being vulnerable, so frequently dismissed in this environment, is part of being human?

Old.   I was once driving around with a real estate agent and referred to an old house we'd seen. The agent looked troubled and a little confused. "I don't think I've shown you any *old* houses," she said in a not-very-friendly way. Then she brightened. "Oh, you mean the *antique* that needs some updating!"

Oops. What a faux pas! Little did I know that "old," when used to describe a house, had become a pejorative. Then again, why not? The adjective "old"—whether you're talking technology, people or anything else—has increasingly come to mean something insulting.

With recent, rapid technological changes, what's new becomes obsolete (read "old") faster than ever before. The "planned" obsolescence of products that early captains of industry envisioned—whoops, you can't get parts for the old one so when it breaks down, you have to buy something new!—has exploded beyond anyone's wildest dreams. Old is mind-numbingly boring, the whiff of something past its prime, the prevention of progress. Old isn't just something that defines length of time; old is bad. And disposable.

The technological link between age and uselessness has spread quickly to other areas. More delicate euphemisms than ever emphasize aspects other than age: think "classic," "traditional" or "vintage" fashion, food brands or cars, skin care products or dog food for the "mature" person or canine, people or pets past a certain age who are "seniors," or the old fixer-upper that becomes a "retro" or "well-loved" home—that is, if it doesn't quite qualify as an antique. Even the vague word "older" (compared to what?) is preferable to old.

"Youth is beauty, beauty, youth," goes the old chestnut celebrated constantly these days. But the real creed in the current climate links the beauty of youth with honor. Which runs counter to Leo Tolstoy's observation from an earlier time: "What a strange illusion it is to suppose that beauty is goodness."

Tolstoy's idea is worth reconsidering today. The theme of the (always) old, ugly, evil witch getting bested by a virtuous young beauty has been around for a long time, but never has it been so frequently hauled out. The tale of the mean old fellow who's

toppled by the young upstart may have existed since an era before Oedipus, but it's amplified in our own. Not only is old undesirable, it's corrupt, cynical, stupid and often vindictive, as
demonstrated on TV: Think of the moral bankruptcy and/or
stupidity of adults on shows ranging from cartoons to *Dawson's
Creek* and MTV. Is it any surprise that the ultimate put-down
in the fashion industry these days is to decree that something
looks "so *mommy*"?

What is old, anyway? That's a tricky question today, with a
great number of people who once wouldn't trust anyone over
thirty now passing fifty themselves. Old may be an attitude—
"I'm much younger than my mother was at my age," is how one
woman in her fifties puts it—but it's almost always linked to appearance as well. Mutton and lamb have gotten all mixed up,
but lamb, invariably, is morally superior.

"Who's Sun Smart?" reads the headline in a recent feature in
a popular women's magazine. "The sun can affect your skin before you even realize it. Here, who has and hasn't learned to
keep herself protected . . ." goes the copy in an issue of *For
Women First*. The tsk-tsk tone of the piece—all it takes is some
sunscreen to look eternally youthful!—is highlighted by
celebrity photos. The sun-damaged Bad Girls are in their forties or older—the fine lines, the article leads you to believe, are
tangible results of their being selfishly sun-dumb. In contrast,
the article gushes over "sun-savvy" celebrities, who, oddly
enough, are unlined twenty-somethings.

Forget that they may be comparing apples with oranges
here, or, to use a more apt metaphor, an aged Beaujolais with
one that's nouveau. Or we could leave the objectification aside
altogether and compare the celebrities profiled as individuals,

viewing them in terms of what they've actually accomplished. Each of the members of one group has at least two decades of work and life experience. None of the others, fresh-faced youngsters, have been in the public eye more than five years. However, everyone is subject to the same scrutiny, and clearly, being lined and old isn't just icky—it's a sin of omission. And it's your own dumb fault, even if you're famous.

Dependent.   Unless you're referring to someone under the age of twenty-one who serves as a tax deduction, "dependent" has increasingly become something to avoid at all costs. In recent years, "co-dependent" has taken on the ominous overtones of drug abuse or worse; to be an "enabler" is to assist someone in destroying their life.

Dependency, even if you don't happen to have the sort of problems that qualify for shock talk shows, has emerged as a sin. Forget that mutual or interdependence might also be called having a relationship or actually being part of a community. And toss aside the notion that a heightened sense of interdependence or connectedness to something outside of ourselves—say, considering the impact of development on the environment—may be beneficial for generations to come.

The single exception this notion of dependence is, naturally, with objects. In a materialized structure, one's own independence is continually signified by objects that one can depend on. Why rely on other unpredictable humans—or your own power—to find satisfaction, when you can "become one with the road" in a new car, feel whole through the "goodness of whole grains," or obtain tranquillity through a bracelet of aura-infused beads? Why shouldn't you depend on your cereal to deliver—especially when you could buy eight boxes for your family of four so everyone can exercise their own independence!

The short answer is that the cereal will probably go stale, and the kids may end up fighting over the toy in one box regardless of how many you buy. The longer answer involves a couple of questions: How much independence can possessions provide? And when does dependence possibly improve one's life?

Fat.   In a land where tolerance for jokes based on ethnicity, race, or gender has plummeted, fat slurs remain fair game. Is it any wonder that 45 percent of Americans surveyed place "getting fat" among their greatest fears? Or that people who are unhappily married are more likely to see their spouses as overweight?

Endlessly reviled, fat is presented as one of the most deadly sins around now. Sure, being overweight isn't especially healthy. But fat has gone beyond health concerns to emerge as a major moral issue, touted to anyone who's even slightly above their ideal weight. Forget pleasingly plump; any fat at all is now positioned as evil, connoting a sort of moral slackness that might be measured in so much cellulite.

As wicked as fat may be, there's an ever-present, odd juxtaposition between having your cheesecake and eating it, too. Anyone who's seen the covers of women's magazines knows they regularly picture mouthwatering, calorie-laden desserts next to taglines for stories that scream about shedding pounds. No-exercise, eat-whatever-you-wish "fat-burning" pills—"consume-more-to-consume-less" solutions—now abound. And have you ever seen anyone remotely massive in ads for Massive-Size fast-food meals? While studies attribute the growing problem of obesity among children and adults in this country to an increase in sedentary activities such as television watching, it may be through those activities that the message of overweight-as-moral-failing—as well as "eat, eat!"—is enunciated.

The attitude that fat itself is somehow demonic has reached new levels in recent years, with some advocates going so far as to call for a federal "sin tax" (like that on tobacco, but here it's called a "fat tax" or "Twinkie tax") to be levied on junk food and calorie-heavy restaurant meals. Interestingly, the call for governmental action against fattening food has, uh, grown proportionally with consumer demand for more: The average weight of a fast-food hamburger has grown from one ounce to four, reflecting studies that restaurant patrons care more than ever about large portion size, according to the National Restaurant Association. (Determining what's "enough" to meet that demand is tough at a time when muffins routinely resemble small hats and a U.S. pasta chain now dishes up *two pounds* of macaroni in a single serving.)

While that single pasta serving may be enough to serve a hungry family of four, the modern-day sin of "fat" is distinct from gluttony, since gluttony is not only tolerated, it's embraced by contemporary culture. (Think of the numerous "shop-till-you-drop" maxims we hear every day, not to mention the myriad diet programs that promise we can actually eat more, more, more—and still lose weight!) And it's separate from old-time sloth, although fat is frequently associated with laziness. Fat is a distinctly contemporary evil because it is all about your appearance supposedly manifesting your ethics and essence. It's not about genetics or metabolism or body type or age: It's about self-respect, managing temptation, and being a happier, better person. Fat is the subject of self-hate, and fat-free is positioned as the object of envy. And clearly, if you're fat, no matter the reason, you're told you've failed.

Average. In Garrison Keillor's made-up town of Lake Wobe-gone, Minnesota, "the women are strong, the men are good-looking, and all the children are above-average." These days, that's not the only place where the mean is avoided. Average isn't good enough. Indeed, average isn't good at all on a con-temporary morality scale.

The demonization of "average" is a relatively recent phe-nomenon. Standardization of everything from measurements of intellectual capabilities to car-safety features to what's al-lowed to go into hot dogs has paved the way for millions of ways to categorize both people and products. In both positive and negative ways, comparisons are now constant in our cul-ture. At the same time, we receive constant messages of hyperreality masquerading as real life along with suggestions of purchasable ways to break free of the middle and move ahead. Consider pseudo poetry on the Marlboro T-shirt that reads:

> *Cowboys still saddle up.*
> *Only today it's not always a sleek stallion.*
> *IT'S A CHOPPER with bright chrome*
> *A LOUD TEMPER*
> *and an unbridled urge to stand out from*
> *THE HERD.*

Hey, who doesn't want to be special? And if you can be out-standing by buying, isn't there a sort of shabby shamefulness in settling for what's simply adequate?

What *is* "adequate," exactly? One of the sharpest and most candid ideological exchanges ever on this issue took place over a humble kitchen table. In 1959 Vice President Richard Nixon arrived in Moscow to meet with Soviet Premier Nikita Khrushchev at the opening of the American National Exhibition, a rare show intended to display American culture to Russians. The low point of the two leaders' already-strained exchange occurred as they stood in the kitchen of a $14,000 model American house: Khrushchev scoffed at the built-in washing machine and other appliances, insisting that the average American didn't need such frivolity—and could never afford it anyway. Nixon, jabbing his finger at the Soviet leader, insisted that any American steelworker could—and did—own a kitchen like the model. This incident kicked off a famous, mudslinging "kitchen debate," where the two leaders argued ideological and national superiority on everything from dishwashers to missiles.

It's been said that Khrushchev's incredulity at Americans' incredibly high "average" standard of living shed a new perspective on what we had, both materially and ideologically. (The "average" home was so elaborate that the leader insisted Nixon was lying, discovering later, of course, that he was not, a source of pride, no doubt, for listeners, viewers, and readers in this country.) Although the "kitchen debates"—and international ideological arguments over dishwashers—are long over, citizens of the United States continue, on average, to possess far more things than citizens of any other nation in the world. But as the ideology of "us" against "them" has waned, so, perhaps, have messages of satisfaction or pride in what we have.

In 1999, the average American earned less than $18,000; the average family, somewhere around $44,000, according to the Bureau of Labor Statistics. However, the presentation of what the "average" person possesses has changed considerably in the last four decades. From watches that sell for what that person earns in a year to sneakers that signify three weeks' take-home salary, material symbols of "the good life" in our culture are depicted as typical and attainable for all. What "everyone" has these days is a far cry from that 1950s kitchen. And it's hardly what most people can truly afford.

The link between "superior products" creating or reflecting "superior people" has placed the "average" person—once considered, well, normal—in the dubious category that political pollsters have dubbed "Joe Six-Pack." Being a regular guy means you're probably missing out on something. Pretty good isn't good enough. Average, in this set-up, is a curse.

Infirm.   One of the more chilling comments I've ever heard came from someone who'd learned an acquaintance had cancer. "But she seemed so healthy. She ate right, she exercised, she didn't use drugs or alcohol. . . ." The woman's voice trailed off. "Still, she must have done *something* that caused her to get sick." That "something" is the sin of fallibility, of terrible, inexplicable luck along the way. However, in a materialized environment, with so many ways to purchase "wellness," infirmity of any sort becomes a moral failing.

Is coffee good or bad for you? Is red wine or yogurt or kelp the key to sturdy longevity? Does one vitamin or another prevent the common cold? Will flossing your teeth prevent heart attacks? (According to the magazine where I read this question, it might. And what a help to see the advertisement for floss just pages away!) Never before has the issue of good health been so hotly debated, so widely promoted, and so seemingly easy to control: in recent years, sales of both over-the-counter and prescription drugs have hit record highs. At the same time, infirmity has never been so demonized: Sickness isn't a matter of chance, but a result of not being on top of things. Did you forget to eat antioxidants and get the flu? In this setup, you failed. And there's no cause but your own shortsightedness.

If infirmity is a sin these days, death is so distasteful that it's pretty much off the radar screen, with a couple of notable exceptions. Certainly, we see and hear frequently about death through the generic victims of formulaic entertainment (someone gets knocked off in the beginning and the heroes spend the next hour dodging bullets; the bad guys get shot in the end) and, of course, in the cavalcade of news stories chronicling aberrant and/or atrocious acts. But nonviolent death—as a natural part of living, as a passage that, inevitably, we're all going to face at some point—isn't part of this picture. Nor is grief. While part of life, death isn't exactly a winning sales concept, and the silence surrounding it in a materialized environment is resounding.

But then, the d-word may become a thing of the past, sort of. Scientists now believe that in the foreseeable future, the whole of a person's experience may be recorded on a microchip implanted in the brain. The developers of the device at British Telecom ambitiously call it the "Soul Catcher"; the idea is that every particle of a person's knowledge, senses, emotions, you name it, will be able to be reproduced and virtually experienced by others long after their body expires. Instant immortality, perhaps—that is, if anyone cares to download your "life." But what of the soul that exists without software? Or, for that matter, without an audience?

In the same space-age vein, others have pushed the idea one step further, believing that not only will a person's being be available on command—it will be capable of continuing to interact with the living. While these technonotions sound a bit wacky, they illustrate an important aspect of materialism-driven culture: You can't take it with you, but there's always the possibility that you'll never have to leave.

Slow.   While you're busy staving off death, though, you'd better not waste any time. Faster, faster, faster has emerged as a mantra in recent years. Speed has become more of the essence than ever. The simmering stove-top stew pot and unattended Crock-Pot have been challenged by the microwave; the wait for the evening paper has become the near-instantaneous delivery of news and other information via the Internet; clunky roller skates of old have evolved into sleek speed machines. The idea, too, of gratification—feeling good, looking good, being good— occurring immediately, and often concurrently, has risen alongside the quest for greater speed.

What's so great about speed? Quite a lot, of course, or we wouldn't seek and buy the things that help provide it. It's hard to remember what it's like to write on a manual typewriter, let alone go back to using one. And most of us would be hard-pressed to give up the convenience, rapidity, and agility—physical and mental—promised, and often delivered, by other innovations of the last couple of decades.

But as things continually speed up, something strange happens: the "gee whiz" wonder at quickness rapidly shifts to wondering why something can't be, well, just a little faster. The baked potato that used to take an hour in the oven now gets zapped in the microwave for about ten minutes—but why isn't it ready in five? Research that once required a trip to the library and hours of thumbing through various sources now arrives on your computer screen in a tiny fraction of the time—but why does it take so long to download? Oh sure, patience is a virtue. But it's hard to cultivate in the current environment.

Slowness of all sorts has become a kind of modern-day enemy, presented, with each higher-speed gizmo, as a sort of roadblock to progress. The technological potential for increased speed implies the capacity to do more; the question of the quality of what's accomplished, however, may fade in the quest for speed.

While we surely do not see ourselves as extensions of machines, expectations of increased speed via objects may have an impact on how we view ourselves and our accomplishments. Speed—even if it doesn't actually improve what you produce or get you what you actually want—is presented as a pressing need. To a great extent, going slowly, in this hierarchy, is shameful, akin to getting left in the dust—or dropping out altogether.

Just as no one confused the Sears Roebuck's 1897 *Consumer's Guide* with the proverbial Good Book back then, it's unlikely that most people these days receive their moral training from the ever-present rumble of media or marketers. Still, why do the modern-day Deadly Sins resonate, even if we know they don't have a lot to do with living ethically? For one thing, they establish simple absolutes—and perhaps, something to aspire to—in a complex world. And for another, we may find a nugget of truth in each of the modern-day Deadly Sins.

Certainly it's not always desirable to be vulnerable or dependent, even if these conditions may be necessary at times for growth in relationships with other people. Infirmity is a drag or worse, even if healing and renewal may emerge from it. The wisdom or beauty that may come with growing old may be less readily apparent than other aspects of the process, no matter how full or deep. As for the sins of being average, fat, or slow, well, there are plenty of real benefits to being special, slender and quick—but is attaining these ideals through objects a matter of morality?

Living Virtues

If we hear a lot about modern sins these days, we also hear about what counts as purchasable saintliness. (Buy a box of cookies and five cents will be contributed to a charity!) Realistically, we know that virtue via objects—doing good by buying well—isn't the same as performing a good deed, with no ulterior motive in mind, for another person. And yet it imbues the act of purchasing with virtue, such as supporting kids in crisis or aiding environmental action. And the material item that's purchased may take on a kind of spiritual goodness.

When the weekly trip down the food aisles at the supermarket becomes an opportunity to "do the right thing," the value of truly ethical behavior may become trivialized. How many times have you heard someone bemoaning being "bad" because they haven't worked out in a while, just ate a brownie, don't know a CD-ROM from RAM, or haven't packed a "healthy" snack or bought the latest "enriching" toy for their child? How often have you felt just a little bit virtuous—at least momentarily— because you have?

Conscience, of course, begins with consciousness of what's right and what's wrong. In *The Origin of Consciousness in the*

Breakdown of the Bicameral Mind, psychologist Julian Jaynes theorizes that early human consciousness may have been a matter of hearing and following hallucinatory "voices." As language developed, he believes early humans heard voices that directed and guided them. The "internal" voice—a leader or god—might give commands to continue working or planting, for example. Sound, Jaynes points out, is "a very special modality. We cannot handle it. We cannot push it away. We cannot turn our backs to it." So powerful is the sense, he points out, that the word "obey" comes from the comes from the Latin *obedire*—"to hear facing someone."

The way we control others' "voice authority" over us, Jaynes explains, is through both our distance from the sound itself and through our opinion of the speaker: "Our personal judgements of others are filters of influence," he writes. In other words, a moral message from Mom probably carries more weight than one from a stranger—or the TV.

Early humans couldn't control this "voice authority"; to hear, Jaynes maintains, was to obey. Consider, he writes, "a voice that you cannot back off from, as close to you as everything you call you, when its presence eludes all boundaries, when no escape is possible—flee and it flees with you—a voice unhindered by walls or distances, undiminished by muffling one's ears, never drowned out with anything, not even one's own screaming—how helpless the hearer!"

Pretty horrifying, no? All those voices early humans may have heard certainly aren't the equivalent of that darn jingle stuck in our heads. Certainly, we have evolved so that we do not feel compelled to obey the voices, internal or external, that we hear. Still, the sounds of materialism-driven morality are tough to escape. The time that we spend hearing those voices, consciously or not, may be huge.

Most of us can't spend all day reading religious tracts, meditating or living lives of solitary, supreme self-sacrifice—nor would we want to. So, short of putting in earplugs and wearing blinders to our environment, what can be done? As one woman I spoke with put it, we can "fight consciousness with consciousness." In other words, separating ourselves from the din of deadly sins in contemporary culture—along with objects to appease them—may mean exploring quieter, but more meaningful virtues.

Just as the Golden Rule appears in one form or another in nearly every religion, the qualities that contribute to being a good person are universal. Acting with compassion and truthfulness toward other people certainly rank among the "right" ways to live across cultures.

What seven—or three, or twenty—virtues are most important to *your* leading a "good" life, as opposed to a packaged image of the "good life"? Because of the high value our culture places on fast, pat, and easy answers, it's not something we're encouraged to ponder very often. And, perhaps, because modern cynicism may twist some traditional definitions of virtue—consider how the notion of "humility" may be interpreted in various, opposing ways these days—clarifying a personal concept of real virtue may be more important than ever.

Extricating the notion of good or bad from objects, then, may mean developing alternatives, not only in consciousness, but in action and experience. What's the right thing to do? For one man who cited kindness as a virtue he tries to live by, it means something as small as letting someone else go ahead of him at a four-way stop sign. To a woman who believes that empathy and patience are important virtues, it means resisting the impulse to snap at her sullen, preadolescent daughter. For another man, who values charity, it means listening to the boring, lonely guy on the train who wants to talk—when he'd much rather read.

One long, dark winter many years ago when my husband and I lived in France, we passed a bloodmobile. My husband, right on the spot, decided that doing something good might do something for the holiday blues we were both feeling, and despite the fact that he spoke almost no French, he climbed aboard to give some blood.

I waited outside for five minutes, and then ten. Five more minutes passed, and I started to get a little nervous. What if something had happened and he couldn't communicate?

A few minutes later, just as I was working up my nerve to go in to investigate, something strange occurred. Loud cheering erupted in the double-decker bloodmobile bus. The happy shouts continued for a few moments, and eventually, my husband emerged from the bus, pale but beaming. A small man followed him out the door and shook his hand happily before he turned to walk off in another direction. As my husband and I started to walk away, two more people descended the steps of the bus to wave and shout "Joyeux Noel!" to my husband.

When I asked about all the noise and the handshake he smiled a bit sheepishly. "They heard I didn't speak French and were happy I was giving blood, so they started cheering." Of course, if he had been in his own country, it wouldn't have happened that way. If he hadn't been with a particularly congenial group of strangers who cared to inquire about him, it wouldn't have been the same. But there, at that moment, he was surrounded by the sound of cheering for a simple act.

Now, real life doesn't generally work the way it does in the movies, where the hero is hailed by strangers. And when the heroism is a tiny act of trying to do something good for its own sake—well, the likelihood of that happening is about once in a lifetime.

Which is, perhaps, why the memory of that moment many years ago is still so strong. The small acts that contribute to others—and contribute to one's own life in turn—are rarely recognized in a public way.

But maybe they're as important as the ones that are. Think back over your own life and you'll probably remember some small, significant good deed from another person—who expected nothing in return—that made a difference in your life. Maybe not a huge difference, but significant enough to remember: the teacher who gave you a break or good advice, the friend who helped without asking questions, strangers who went out of their way to be kind. And perhaps you can remember something you did, small and seemingly unnoticed, that someday, someone else will recall as well.

A saying that's been around for a while now advocates practicing "random acts of kindness" and "senseless acts of beauty." It's a lovely idea. But here's another thought: in an era where conscience is questioned and assuaged through the ever-present answer of objects, perhaps we need to be a bit more deliberate. At a time when acts of goodness are constantly linked to buying the right item, consciousness of how goodness truly happens needs to break through the noise of authoritative voices and become top-of-mind.

The strong appeal of objects as a moral answer comes from the surety of the messages we receive. The opportunity to do something good is all set up and ready to go with a purchase; the desire has an unambivalent response in the form of a possession. And so, perhaps, the decision to *actually* do the right thing must be just as deliberate. Okay, maybe we can't go as far as the cartoon Boy Scout urging the unwilling little old lady across the street. But looking out for opportunities to act in kindness and with beauty, not randomly or senselessly, but with purpose, may help to answer the desire to do the right thing— in a way that lasts longer than the "right" purchase. And it may even trigger something my father calls a "virtuous circle"—as opposed to a vicious cycle.

The willingness to seek ways to do something good violates at least one of the modern-day Deadly Sins, that of vulnerability. The outcome is unknown. The stakes may be high. The "self" is put on the back burner. This kind of exposure—to rejection, ungratefulness, even possible hostility—requires great courage. It means taking a risk. And it's certainly not a sure bet that doing something good will pay off personally in any way at all.

But, according to those who have tried it, the odds aren't bad. A teenager who spent two weeks building a clinic for disadvantaged people told me, "I could move away from my own stupid worries." A woman who works as a mentor to a needy child says of the experience, "It's frustrating sometimes. But even when our time together doesn't go well, I know I've tried. And when it does go well, there's nothing like it."

Grace/Dis-Grace

Sin is tied to a fall from grace, of course, and doing good is said to be an act of grace. So what's actually disgraceful? Throughout history, objects have absorbed the moral overtones of their times: Think of the Victorians hastening to drape furniture with fabric, lest the sight of a bare piano leg provoke licentious thoughts. While the aesthetics of morality are in constant flux, the idea that objects communicate propriety—remember the line about the importance of wearing clean, intact undergarments in case you get hit by a car?—remains. A state of disgrace may result from failing to do something, or doing something wrong, but it's also tied into the idea of objects doing something on their own. And certainly, it makes sense, to some extent: Ensuring that your child has clothes, enough to eat, and a stable place to live is essential, whether defined as a moral or material imperative.

Still, what's presented as "essential" is ever-shifting in our culture, and the threat of disgrace that's a result of *not* having may get distorted, like looking into one of those carnival mirrors that messes up how we see ourselves. In that strange mirror, not buying your child this year's top-of-the-line brand may mesh with neglect, "enough" to eat becomes an ode on the snack pack, and the stable place to live morphs into owning the toys, electronics, and anything else that promises your child will maintain a competitive edge among peers. With this distortion, the pit of possible disgrace from not possessing something is ever-widening, ready to be filled with objects.

While the threat of disgrace is enunciated often, the notion of grace itself is a lot harder to pin down. Which may explain why it doesn't get a whole lot of play these days. In a spiritual sense, grace might be defined as an unexpected gift, something that arrives, unasked-for and unearned. In theological terms, divine grace helps, saves, and can offer redemption. And whether grace is framed by religion or not, it's belief in something we get that we may have no business getting, something wonderful that may happen for no good reason. It blows in and delivers what you want or need, even if you never knew you wanted it. It's goodness that can't be compared or explained. It just is. It just happens.

Because grace arrives in as many ways as there are individuals, the goodness of grace defies anything finite, purchasable, tangible. Because it is something that may have an effect but no cause, a result but no finish line, grace may be hard to recognize at times. So, perhaps at the core of finding grace is the ability to be, well, grateful. For grace to happen, it's got to be recognized.

Gratitude isn't exactly promoted in the current environment. Although technological advances of the past century provide some sort of material perspective on the past and anticipation of the future—see how slow, difficult and/or backwards things were back then and how much more they'll soon improve!— there's little external focus on the intangible things we have in the present. Experiencing grace, then, may be discovering what you have. It may mean fulfillment that happens when you aren't trying to have more, and when you don't expect it.

A woman I spoke with described grace as something that the world presents as an offering, which you can either accept or ignore: "When I was going through a bad period in my life, I finally decided I needed to take a 'misery vacation.' I forced myself to pay attention to what I had instead of what I was missing. I had a choice: I could see the old window on my house that needed cleaning or I could notice the beautiful way the light played in the leaves of the trees outside. I could choose to feel irritated by the old window or be grateful for what I was able to see through it."

I once heard an irritating person described this way: "He doesn't see the glass as half-full or half-empty, but looks inside and never sees what he wants to drink, so he sends it back. It's never right." Grace, perhaps, is working to see the glass as half-full—and trying to have compassion for those who can't. And maybe part of working toward living in grace is to live with the knowledge that while all is not right with the world, and there are often wrong drinks and cruel people and unfair events and things you want and likely will never have, *something* is right, and that what you do have is worthy of notice and thanks.

While grace may just happen, the moment of recognizing grace, of finding the gift of the dappled light in the leaves or in the way your child laughs with pure hilarity or in the sweet smell of the air after a long rain, is a conscious act. And sometimes, said one man I spoke with, it requires work. "I have to make myself switch focus. When I'm feeling that I have nothing to feel good about, I ask myself, if I could be a mindful sort of person, what would I notice right now? If I act as if I *could* be grateful, it helps me become more grateful."

A social worker once told me about a daily exercise, used in recovery programs, which seems to make sense for almost anyone. "Find the gift of your day and reflect on it," she said. "It could be as fundamental as still being alive or being able to breathe or walk or hear or see. But the gift is there. Acknowledge it."

8

⌣∶∾

BEING BETTER

*You may find that because of one thing or another, you are
limited to building a smaller ramp or quarterpipe rather
than the monumentally tall and wide structure you
originally had your heart set on. Don't be discouraged.
Use what you can and ride what you've got.*

—THRASHER SKATEBOARD MAGAZINE, "SKATEBOARD RAMPS MANUAL"

Size Matters. Sure, it's only the tagline for the 1998 version of
the film *Godzilla*, but its meaning applies to more than mon-
sters in our culture. Bigger—along with stronger, faster,
smarter, happier—makes a difference, and the desire to become better, to have *more,* and perhaps to see your children
surpass your own accomplishments is ingrained in the American Dream and American life. Who doesn't want to rise to
meet a challenge? Then again, why does the ongoing and often
difficult process of becoming better get confused in our culture
with buying something?

If you learn just one thing from materialism-driven values,
it's this: Objects don't just reflect achievement, they're key to it.
Being "better" isn't just measured in the brands you buy; suc-

cess may depend on them. Sure, we hear stories about bare-foot champion runners and home-run slugger Sammy Sosa not having a real baseball mitt until he hit the big time. But for every modern miracle story of becoming better through talent, hard work, and determination, we receive multiple messages of another, much easier way to get there that involves buying something.

Does it ever work? Well, of course it does; it's certainly easier to catch a ball with a mitt, and having one that's softer, suppler, and fits just right might make a difference. Our susceptibility to the magical promise of becoming better through stuff isn't always just wishful thinking. Still, how far does it go?

The link between owning "better" objects and a state of somehow *being* better is about comparison and competition, success made manifest. Take the case of the film publicist I once worked for who graded the cards on her voluminous Rolodex with a red pen. The "A" list were stars of the stars, the most important in the industry. The "B" list folks, naturally, were less important and therefore, less desirable. That left those tentatively clinging to her "C" list, people who perhaps once had some showbiz success, or knew someone who did. Finally, there were people she deemed unworthy of any grade at all—in this publicist's caste system, "room-fillers." If you dropped below that level, she chucked your card.

Given the mercurial nature of success in the movie business, those grades constantly fluctuated. One breakthrough role was enough to turn a room-filler into an "A." A couple of flops could send someone in a rapid downward spiral, if not out altogether.

For the publicist, annual gifts became a sort of social and business barometer to let recipients know how she thought they were doing. It was a task she relished, Grinchishly telling falling or rising stars in the industry where they ranked. The year I worked for her, she spent hours choosing various kinds of date books to give as gifts. Her gradations between types of leather, styles, including a pen or not—along with the elaborateness of gift wrap—got so complicated that simple As, Bs, and Cs wouldn't do. Pluses or minuses were added; last-minute flops meant just-in-time downgrades. Minute gradations—not to mention hours of shopping—made the gamut of items run from vaunted ostrich to dreaded vinyl, the ultimate put-down in her mind.

Never mind that most of the people on her lists probably preferred to buy their own date books, and that her gift would end up in the garbage or as a stocking stuffer for someone else. Forget that her message would likely be lost on the gift recipients. It gave her great glee to believe that each date book clearly carried her thought. And that the thought—maliciously condescending or smarmily ingratiating—would actually count to those she wanted to reach.

While we probably don't "grade" people or objects in the same way, more expensive objects may carry more meaning for more people. It's hard to know where the authentic desire to become better and the burden to buy "better" begins and ends, but in the current environment, the connection between the two may be stronger than ever. Here are some ideas as to why:

The rise of "Celebutantes," or How to Succeed Without Really Trying.   If you had to name the restaurant that best reflects current American culture, what would it be? A fast-food chain?

An all-you-can-eat buffet? One that may not immediately spring to mind but bears mentioning is Tinseltown Studios, the late-1990s California theme restaurant. With employees posing as screaming fans, aggressive reporters and paparazzi, patrons didn't just get a meal—they got to be a celebrity for the night! The $45.00 prix fixe menu included dinner, participation in a fictitious "Awards Show," and, of course, all the attention from strangers that one could demand.

Sure, this one-night debut of would-be celebrities—"celebutantes"—may have been harmless fun. But it also reflects the increasing focus on fame—forget why you're being celebrated—as a goal. It's not simply that most Americans could name the actors on *ER* sooner than they could recall the name of our Surgeon General. It's about hyped-up image itself becoming something exalted, and, possibly, presented as something attainable for all.

Do we really believe famous people are "better"? Maybe not, but attaining fame, if only for a few minutes, seems to be a national lust. When being better gets quantified through the number of people paying attention to you—they know your name but you don't know theirs—an ordinary existence can seem pretty, well, ordinary.

But then, opportunities for playing the part of a "celebutante" abound in our culture. You can always buy something imbued with the spirit of a celebrity; you can create the same "look" you see on television; you can acquire the image through stuff. It's not the same as actually becoming better, or really accomplishing something that might lead to self-recognition or any other kind, of course, but hey, what did you expect?

Cynicism and consumption.   National character may not be shaped by television characters, and image hasn't yet overtaken substance, but in recent years, it seems that something has sunk in about betterment through purchasing power. In 1974, 34 percent of college students believed making lots of money was the key to happiness; that number has jumped to 75 percent nearly thirty years later. And while 70 percent of students once believed that developing a philosophy of life was important, now only about 40 percent do.

Perhaps every generation has believed they were somehow "better" than those who follow them—less apathetic, less cynical—but these themes seem to have come up increasingly in recent years. Conversely, perhaps every generation believes that the ones who preceded them had something important to discover—or fight for or against—that no longer exists.

Certainly, part of this perception may be shaped by the finite nature of images. A student of mine, writing about the 1960s, sincerely believed that the entire decade was one long, groovy, bell-bottomed love-in. On a more sinister note, the narrator of Alex Garland's *The Beach* seeks to find a kind of final frontier in the form of an untouristed, unspoiled beach in Thailand. His quest is informed by images from movies about the Vietnam War; his own sense of reality, in searching for something authentic, gets increasingly confused with "reality" from films. With dire results.

What does this have to do with becoming better? The desire to make the authentic discovery or really change the world exists alongside an infinite number of images and information that says it's all been done before. The cynical translation? There's little left to produce, but much to consume.

And it may be more common than ever. With more messages answering the desire to produce with the act of consuming, the link between becoming better and purchasing something may tighten. You might never find that uncharted island or philosophy of life, but at least one thing is certain: you can still buy the bell-bottoms.

The rise in purchasable perfection.   When young Americans stitched samplers hundreds of years ago, they probably made some genuine mistakes. But often, say textile historians, they deliberately included some small fault—a break in the pattern, a color that was slightly off—to demonstrate humility. The idea was that your work couldn't hope to compete with divine perfection, or perhaps that of your elders. Imperfection is part of what makes those works so charming. And it's a far cry from the present approach to "perfect."

If "better" makes the heart beat faster, then the ever-present prospect of perfection could just about do us in these days. "Picture-perfect" as an attainable goal has hit everything from golf games to office design to relationships. Of course, this concept of perfection doesn't take into account the temporality of taking a picture; the idea is that objects can create perfection that endures and is capable of touching all aspects of your life.

Which doesn't exactly promote the idea of contentment with what you have. When perfection is presented as something that's always possible, "better" is never adequate.

One-upping the world.   Who cares what the Joneses own? You may not, but somebody does.

Who doesn't know someone—a relative or someone you might even like sometimes—who one-ups with objects? You know who I'm talking about. If you have a new grill, they mention one that's more efficient. If you're happy with your old kitchen, they outline how much you're missing by not having one like theirs.

It doesn't take particular insight to grasp that endless comparison with objects is a lost cause, since there will always be a bigger grill, a newer kitchen, and another something to buy that's better. Enough, with this attitude, always means just a little more, and is always in relation to what other people have.

These comparisons do not make for great conversation. They don't pave the way for sharing anything deeper than a description of the last purchase—or inspiring anything more meaningful than resentment or irritation. And yet, when we keep hearing that an external display of possessions indicates inner superiority, it's not especially surprising.

"What 1% of the world wants, it gets," the car ad challenges. The choice of acquisition becomes a mad, competitive dash between you and the rest of the world, if not the universe. Be better by buying, it's saying, or include yourself among the poor slobs who never get what they want.

But what is it that the 1 percent—or for that matter, the other 99 percent—really want? It's easy to dismiss competition in consumption as an increasingly gnawing need to impress. While the superficial "I'm just as good, if not better, than you" may come through via objects, it's probably not top-of-mind when we decide to buy. After all, who's going to admit to themselves, or to anyone else, that they care deeply about "status"? Among other things, it's un-American.

But they care about survival. And when ownership of something "better" is positioned as a kind of lifeboat keeping you from the depths of downward mobility, climbing aboard becomes pretty compelling, as does keeping the sharks at bay.

The predators that circle in contemporary culture may be imagined or blown way out of proportion, but the desire to be better endures. Who doesn't want, in some way, to become better not only in comparison to others but in our hearts? It doesn't take much more than common sense to understand that having the best isn't doing your best, and that becoming better at doing something doesn't magically happen because you buy something. Still, it can seem that way.

Talent in the Tools

How do we dematerialize becoming better—so it can actually happen?

Several years ago, I came across a newspaper article on storage. Now, as someone who is not the world's best housekeeper, (to put it mildly), this looked interesting. If I had a place to put everything, I thought, then I wouldn't have all that mail piling up on the counter.

Lost in this pleasant daydream, I turned the page to a layout of handsome standing cabinets. "Don't you feel more creative imagining your crafts materials in *this* armoire?" crowed the caption. Here was the ticket, I thought. Maybe if I got all those bits of fabric out of the plastic bags they're stuffed in and into some kind of order in an armoire, I'd actually feel inspired to find time to start the quilt I planned to do a decade ago. The clutter, somehow, would also disappear from the rest of my house. The armoire would multitask for me—I'd be a better housekeeper and more creative to boot!

Imagining those clear counters and a lovely handmade quilt in some fantasy future was nearly enough to make me remove the sleeping cat draped over the telephone and order the armoire right then and there. Figuring out where I'd actually put the thing in my crowded house, not to mention how I was going to pay for it, didn't figure into my thinking. And forget considering just how it was actually going to improve my clutter-reduction skills, summon the creative muses, or really make me make something.

I'll admit that it didn't take much to get me going. A few grainy photos and a little uplifting copy and I was off.

Often, you don't even need to make the connection yourself. Talent, we hear constantly, is in the tools: the athletic shoes that pump up your jump shot, the computer that promises better grades, or the professional-quality baking pan that will turn out professional-quality cookies, to name a few. Commitment to the cause gets articulated in how much you're willing to commit to the product. If you really take your pursuit seriously, you should be happy to shell out for it, whatever it takes.

And while we're besieged by messages that link the triumph of champions—and the seriousness of their excellence—to a product, the connection we make to transforming our own lives is, perhaps, the most powerful. Talent in shooting hoops may be up for sale, but it becomes more compelling when you care about the jump shot—and can't quite seem to make it. The armoire may have no meaning until you put it in the personal context of wanting to be better organized—or say, more creative.

Like originality, passion, and perseverance, creativity is a quality you can't buy, of course. Still, the promise of obtaining creativity through objects—"express yourself!"—is particularly potent. Shopping is not creation, as *Generation X* author Douglas Coupland noted, but it may feel like it—for a while. The desire, not only to become better, but to do something original, unique, even profound gets presented through material "fresh starts": a makeover, new wallpaper, a computer that advocates "think different." Sure, there's some creativity involved in putting different material elements together. But let's get real. How often does it lead to thinking "different" or doing something original?

I'd like to be able to say that after I abandoned the idea of the armoire, I sprang off the couch, cleaned up the clutter, and whipped out the pinking shears to make that quilt. It would be great to say that I suddenly recognized my burning desire to be a better housekeeper or become more creative with those fabric scraps—and actually did something about it. No such luck. Instead, I turned the page.

But while my counters were still just as cluttered—and still are, to this day—my brief dream of an armoire did make me start considering, well, alternatives. What does being better really mean? And what's it worth?

Product versus Process

I once heard a story from a young man who asked a painter how he could stand selling his work after spending so much time and energy creating his canvases. The young man knew this was how the painter made a living, but felt unsettled by the idea of the artist parting with work that had demanded so much of him. The painter said he sometimes kept his work, but more often he didn't care much—actually, he was grateful—when he sold something. "It's the process that matters, and I keep that," he told the young man.

The young man telling me the story was surprised, and a little confused. "Maybe they pay him so much that he can't refuse," he said. The storyteller had never thought much about process, he admitted. Then again, before hearing the story I hadn't either.

Certainly, very little in our culture prepares us to consider process over product. Almost from babyhood, we learn about achievement and goals, about the reward at some definite end. Later, we may view ourselves as "products" of our environments or "arriving" at some endpoint. In the meantime, our eyes are trained on the prize: the "A" on the report card, the winner's cup at the end of the season, the high price our work may command someday. Sure, we may hear about perseverance and discipline and other elements that make up the process of becoming better at something, but the product—and where we rank, along with what we have to show for it at the end of the day—is what we're trained to see.

Naturally enough. Process, on the other hand, can be painful (think of someone practicing violin the first few times, for example), frustrating, discouraging, and boring. But it can also be exhilarating. Still, unless you happen to go through it yourself or are a first-hand witness to process, product usually steals the show. Product is the winning photo finish, the award clanking around your neck, the delighted acceptance to the college of your choice. Process may be essential to everything from being a better jump-roper to building a better relationship, but the product gets the applause and roses at the end of the show.

And unlike the sometimes-amorphous, digressive way of process, with product there *is* always an end to the show. Afterwards, it's onward and upward, to the next goal, role, or prize.

Product-centeredness is orderly, rational, twisting a bit, perhaps, but basically linear. Like the board game of Life in which you tool in a tiny car through the hills and valleys of a plastic landscape, acquiring a spouse, kids, and possessions along the way—the process is equated to the products you collect and add up at the end. Although real life isn't quite so straightforward—potholes and the road less traveled have a way of appearing—benchmarks, goals, and tangible rewards are part of the way we live.

And, perhaps, now more so than ever. Certainly, the process of living and learning doesn't hold a blue ribbon at every turn, but objects increasingly represent accomplishment, any accomplishment. Take trophies, now a prominent feature of little kids' sports, which are awarded to all for just getting through the season. From around age five, shiny gold statuettes go to those who actually engaged in the process of playing and those who didn't. Far be it from me to deny some little kid his shiny metal soccer player, but it's an interesting contemporary symbol. The pleasure of just kicking around a ball for a couple of hours a week, it seems, isn't enough anymore. A tangible award punctuates the end of the season.

Since the power of the product is so seductive, the process may get lost somewhere. A fairly common modern definition of success is the acquisition of more, the transition from good to better to "best." The house gets an addition; another car is acquired; a bigger house starts to look a lot better; and maybe there's a pool or a boat or something else to consider. Because it's nice to have more space and a pool would be fun, too—this pure, product-oriented approach seems to make sense.

"The squalid cash interpretation put on the word success. . . is our national disease," wrote the theologian William James, in a letter to H. G. Wells way back in 1906. The problem is that process may get short shrift in the quest for tangible "more" success—money, objects or emotional fulfillment. Just like the boxes in the board game, it doesn't allow much time for contemplation or taking stock of other things or acceptance of experience for its own sake. With a constant focus on future "better"—in material or any other terms—it's hard to see the merit in the moments that make up the present.

A comment I've heard frequently in affluent suburbs about teenagers driving expensive cars reflects parental concern: *If they get a sports car at the age of seventeen, what do they have to look forward to?* But it also illustrates the limitations of product-centered thinking.

Not long ago, a high-school student shared a story about a discussion in his English class about a tragic double suicide that had been reported in the news. The victims were good-looking rich kids, with closetfuls of designer-of-the-day clothing, lots of disposable cash, and long lists of accomplishments (with, no doubt, the trophies to back them up), along with acceptances to coveted colleges.

One of the kids also possessed a brand-new sports car, which he intentionally used to drive himself and his girlfriend off a cliff to their agreed-upon deaths. In the note they left they said they had gotten everything they'd ever wanted and had no reason to continue going on with living. The student told me the majority of his high-school classmates reacted to the story with feigned ennui, cool detachment, and a pretense of understanding: The kids had everything already, the group reasoned. What else *did* they have to live for?

Two brief lives were reduced to a pile of possessions. When "something to look forward to" gets translated into "something 'better' to buy," the sanctity of life, the continuum of experience, the process of living and learning, including both good times and bad, may somehow get summed up in acquiring one product after another.

Becoming "better" may involve pain and compromise and acceptance. But considering the process of becoming better over some imaginary finish line—or trophy—may help turn the question of "is that all there is?" to an engagement in what *is*, good or bad. And it may open us up to an awareness of something larger and more lasting than the next notch up, the next prize, the next ending.

Psychologist Mihalyi Csikszentmihalyi calls this process of engaging "flow," or "optimal experience." Achieving flow involves setting goals, concentration, and a sense of purpose— pursuing something for its own sake, and not for some future prize. When experiencing this kind of engagement, he writes in *Flow: The Psychology of Optimal Experience*, "people become so involved in what they are doing that the activity becomes spontaneous, almost automatic; they stop being aware of themselves as separate from the actions they are performing."

Does engaging in process make one "better" at something? Possibly. But more important, it can bring more enjoyment and satisfaction to what we do, "better" or not.

A man who's a good, competitive athlete told me he took up roller blading in his mid-thirties. Awkward at first, then gaining proficiency, he finally felt ready to try roller hockey. When he started, he said, nearly everyone in his pickup game was younger than him and more skilled at the sport. But this time he decided not to keep score with himself while playing a competitive game.

After three years, he said, he's improved. "I'm finally playing a sport without worrying about the next win. It's great to play well, and I'm still not crazy about doing badly in a game. But I've found I get more out of just playing—being aware of getting a pass just right, getting the feeling of flying when I'm going after the puck—than in all those years of having to win."

Product can always be compared to others. It's often tangible. It's immediately identifiable and easy to grasp, from the Good Conduct Medal to the bonus check at the end of the year. It's a victory, even if it only lasts until the next marking period.

Process, on the other hand, keeps going. It can't be quantified or reproduced. And because it exists only between an individual and experience, the rewards are unique and internal. And last, perhaps, far longer than any trophy.

What's "Better"?

With so much stuff out there that promises easy improvement, the "process" of becoming—becoming better or becoming anything else—may get lost. With so many purchasable ways to acquire "perfection," the time, energy, and concentration required to *actually* engage in activity may get diffused. Maybe we don't necessarily fritter away the time we could devote to, say, becoming a better runner by dreaming about jogging suits. But all those messages on the pursuit of buying "better" can distract us from what we really want to achieve.

You could look at yard sales as an afternoon's worth of free entertainment—I know I have. On the other hand, if you feel like playing detective, you could see them as a kind of cultural meter, a personal record of abandoned pursuits, or a place where the half-life of hope persists. The mismatched free weights, unused yogurt makers, and barely begun craft kits may not signify reproach—but they may tell a story. And perhaps yard sales beckon because one person's discarded dream is another's treasure of possibility: With the bargain in hand, you might become the kind of person who works out regularly, makes her own yogurt, and finishes something she starts.

Then again, you might not. What do you wish to become? With so many options for improvement, the priority may get masked. Which might lead to a leap of belief that an armoire is all it takes to become a person who regularly clears off the counters.

Sorting out the confusion between "having" and actually "doing" may require a rethinking of the time that truly engaging requires. How important is changing that aspect of your life for you, really? How much will the object do, realistically, to effect that change? What can you live with in yourself? What's intolerable?

Since ownership is linked to improvement, it's worth considering an old notion from the poet Dante: Possession is one with loss. The charming old rooms in a house may get dwarfed and made shabby by the new addition, and the video game may cut into reading time. Or on another level, buying a size-sixteen dress may wipe out the fantasy and hope of wearing a size ten.

So, what's gained in possession? What's lost? Perhaps it's worth considering the dematerialized idea that "better" may not lie in a bigger house or a smaller dress size. And it might be worth looking at what might get lost–of ourselves and our potential for, well, achieving some kind of greatness—with faith in possessions to make it happen.

Reinventing Better: Affirming Action

We live in an environment that fervently believes in the "best of all possible worlds" that Voltaire's Candide seeks—and never finds. Instead, he ends up cultivating his own small garden. And perhaps that's a place to start in the quest for "better."

"How'm I doing?" It's a question schools seem to be asking themselves these days, through an increased focus on standardized testing. At the same time, the theory of "multiple intelligences"—the idea that humans have a broad variety of strengths that may not be reflected in traditional intelligence tests—as developed by Dr. Howard Gardner, has also gained attention. The two, of course, aren't mutually exclusive, since the process of learning presumably leads to the product of high scores.

Ask taxpaying parents what they care about and, reasonably enough, chances are they'll go for the "proof" of high scores. Still, the acceptance of diverse intelligence and ways of learning—and attempting to work to meet the needs of individual students—is a nod to process. There's more than one way to skin a cat—or learn something.

While test scores have emerged as the bottom line on "better" education, they don't, of course, convey all that kids have learned—or haven't. They don't, necessarily, motivate anyone to actually want to learn more. Or teach better.

Test scores are the way of our world, of course, and external recognition—good, bad, or indifferent—counts for quite a lot. Whether you agree with judgments surrounding a single test or coat you wear, there's very little you can do about it. However, you can do something about developing another approach to becoming better alongside the one that already exists.

Perfection may be found in the best of all possible test scores, but it's hard to wrap your head around it in the rest of life. When we keep hearing that perfection is a reasonable, attainable goal—with possessions to help you along, of course—anything less may be a bit disappointing. It doesn't mean you can't keep searching, of course. But the problem is that you may never get any closer to what you seek.

So perhaps the first step in actually working toward becoming better is to abandon the idea of "perfect" so endlessly enunciated in our culture. And the shift from the endless dream of "best" to living as work-in-progress, perhaps, involves figuring out what's worth a commitment—and what isn't. We hear that the right tools can make nearly anything happen; that the "better" object will bring us closer to multiple goals. So where do you actually want to devote your time to make it happen? How important is it to you? And how unhappy does not being "better" at something make you feel?

I'm embarrassed to admit there was a dreadful moment on my twenty-fifth birthday when I actually sat down and mourned what I hadn't yet accomplished, and likely would not, in my life. The list, in retrospect, was absolutely laughable: At that ripe old age, I sadly realized that I'd probably never dance in "The Nutcracker." (Never mind that I'd never once considered seriously studying ballet before that day.) I'd never publish a novel before the age of twenty-five. (Not that I'd ever tried to write one.) I'd never be a prodigy. (Something, I can honestly say, I'd never even considered before or after that day.) I could go on with every missed opportunity I identified on that gloomy day, but it's making me cringe, so I won't.

Lounging on the dark couch of youthful self-pity many years ago, I was briefly incapable of noting anything that I actually had accomplished. Or of noticing what I had at the time that could aid in whatever I hoped to achieve: a great family, a happy marriage, a good education, a healthy body. In mourning what I hadn't yet done, I failed to recognize what I might yet do if I actually got up and starting doing it.

It would be nice to say that my list of nonachievements included some altruistic accomplishment, say, privately aspiring to be a better person in the world, à la Mother Teresa. Forget about it. Instead (I'm cringing again) it was all about outside recognition: the fantasy thunder of applause or a possible mention in a magazine. And at such a young age!

Golly. Recognition from the world, of course, is a nice thing. But perhaps the place where recognition has to start is in working to see the benefits of the process of becoming as it happens, as opposed to bemoaning the fact that the product isn't there yet. It's the care and cultivation of the garden instead of the bouquet at the end of the growing season.

It's not only about stopping and smelling the proverbial roses, though on that long-ago birthday, I could certainly have used that insight, however corny. It's about affirming action, acknowledging the tiny pieces of "better" in what you do. Far from grandiose fantasy as enunciated by the double entendre advertisement for fur coats featuring celebrities—asking, "What Becomes a Legend Most?"—it's about looking at becoming, not through a coat or as a legend, but in living.

Acknowledgment of small, incremental steps that add up to larger accomplishment doesn't sit very well with a culture where finish lines keep moving. If you took a picture of someone engaging in activity, it might not seem like much next to the grand symbols of success we see so frequently. Though it might not look like a lot— there's triumph in finishing the crossword puzzle even if nobody else notices—it means something. And making an effort to recognize the steps in the process may lead to a sense of greater satisfaction along the way.

What's more, it might yield fewer regrets. The threat of not becoming "better" is a disappointed "worse"; the expectation of onward and upward may set us up for a bigger fall when it doesn't happen. Valuing the experience of engaging—good or bad—for its own sake may put "better" into broader perspective, removed from finite rewards or targets.

In Edgar Lee Masters's *Spoon River Anthology*, Fiddler Jones, like other characters in the poetry collection, speaks from the grave about his life. In direct contrast to the fable of the Ant and the Grasshopper (the industrious-but-dull ant survives, the charming-but-lazy grasshopper bites the dust) or Horatio Alger's heroes (those poor-but-industrious fellows who worked tirelessly, lived frugally, and ended up with vast riches in the end) the fiddler tells us how he just, well, lived. But not without great riches or success of a different sort.

He says, by way of introduction, "The earth keeps some vibration going, / There in your heart, and that is you." His own vibration is music; his livelihood is in farming forty acres. He's cheerfully unsuccessful at the pursuit, he says, for

> *How could I till my forty acres,*
> *Not to speak of getting more,*
> *With a medley of horns, bassoons and piccolos*
> *Stirred in my brain by crows and robins*
> *And the creak of a windmill—only these?*

The fiddler "never started to plow in my life, / When someone did not stop in the road / And take me away to a dance or a picnic" where he would play his violin. He survives until he is ninety; he never acquires more land or becomes a better farmer. But, he says,

> *I ended up with forty acres*
> *I ended up with a broken fiddle—*
> *And a broken laugh, and a thousand memories,*
> *And not a single regret.*

It's not really the American Dream. But all told, it doesn't get much better than that.

9

❦

FREE FROM FEAR

Present fears
Are less than horrible imaginings. . .

—WILLIAM SHAKESPEARE, *MACBETH*

Your brakes may fail on the highway during the thunderstorm, hurtling you and your kids into oblivion. The food you're eating could contain toxic chemicals or bacteria. Dangerous germs can lurk in every corner of your house. Scary people may be among your neighbors. Malevolent aliens might be out there but unseen, waiting for the moment to strike and destroy.

Be afraid. Be very afraid. In a climate of consumption, which futurist Faith Popcorn calls "atmos-fear," more information than ever identifies reasons to be afraid and things to buy to alleviate those fears. But what can they do for a fundamental sense of never quite feeling safe?

Were the dangers of the forest in the past any less hazardous than the possible danger that might await your child in the form of a creepy guy on the playground? Were threats to survival in the Dark Ages less serious than those in an Information Age?

It's hard to say. What's clear, however, is that the perception of possible danger has sharpened dramatically in the last thirty years. Despite steady declines in crime in recent years, 70 percent of Americans believe that crime rates are on the rise. That view, as well as worries about natural disasters, financial calamities, ruinous illness, and personal accidents, has resulted in a doubling of safety-related purchases since the 1970s.

Why are people so worried? Certainly, reasons to be fearful are more widely and clearly articulated than ever. While ignorance may be less stressful, generally, it's not an option. Faster and in greater numbers than ever, we learn about terrible events and inhumane acts and possible danger, both to our quality of life as well as to our lives themselves.

The media, of course, plays a key role. With near-instant access, we now receive information on everything from a devastating earthquake in Istanbul to a shooting in the next state over, from an outbreak of a rare illness in a faraway African provincial city to a violent crime in our own neighborhood. Its scope, along with its rapid-fire pace, may make this fear-inducing information tougher than ever to process.

With so little downtime between horrifying images and stories, panic, anger and a near-blind desire to protect ourselves from similar fates may be the knee-jerk reaction. And there may be another, equally horrifying story right behind it. So little time to reflect on that initial reaction—and actually process, in a reasonable way, what scary events really mean in our own lives, and what we can do about them—may contribute to a heightened state of anxiety.

A common theory about the effect on children of watching violence on television and in movies claims young minds are unable to process images of ugly acts. A scary image stays with them, remaining in their minds without context, goes the argument. When children can't edit realistic and terrifying images, they may have a harder time discerning between what is real and what is simply a scary story. Seeing violent acts again and again, researchers warn, may anesthetize children's ability to feel, respond, or separate the image they see from reality.

Is it a great leap of reason to wonder if the same problem affects us as adults? And is it possible that we suffer a pervasive sense of fear simply through repeated exposure to images of violence and suffering? "Cruelty and fear shake hands together," wrote Honoré de Balzac more than a hundred years ago—and it is still true today. Given the volume and pace of violent images in our lives, our ability to place horrifying events into a realistic and meaningful context may be impaired.

Era of Fear

The enemy you know may be no less threatening than the one at large and unseen, but at least you have some idea of what you're up against. Far-off ideological fear-with-a-face—images of dreadful breadlines, colorless landscapes, and cheerless servitude to an oppressive government—that may have somehow united Americans in the past has changed, of course. Since the perceived communist threat to our way of life has gone the way of the dismantled Berlin Wall and backyard bomb shelters, the good guys/bad guys distinctions aren't quite as simple.

In their place, perhaps, we hear about threats of a far more diverse and personal nature: No longer us against them, it's every person for himself against a multitude of ideological, biological, psychological, and physical enemies. If you're unprepared, you could be the next victim.

And that threat may now be closer than you think. The seemingly mild-mannered fellow who transforms into a monster lurked long before Dr. Jekyll and Mr. Hyde appeared in Robert Louis Stevenson's 1886 novel, but recently, he's come into his own. The scariest terrors aren't straightforward ghouls, but the sneaky, fool-the-eye kind: the devastating, mysterious illness that, at first, looks like a simple cold; the pillar of the community who's actually abusive; the safe haven of home that's filled with hidden toxins. It's that element of contradiction and surprise—who would have thought?—that frames the inexplicable and makes it drama. In the last thirty years, the increasing use of that drama—news events made into a "story" for purposes of entertainment or information, isolated incidents or, say, medical studies pieced together and presented as a "trend"— may have an impact on our perception of danger.

You are there: The villain, in these dramas, isn't in some far-off place but might be hiding in your own neighborhood, your school, or even in your own body. Over the last thirty years, the evils of disease and dysfunction get credited with the possibility of overpowering us at any time. Chalk it up to greater awareness of these issues or the sales of sensationalism; whatever the cause, the dangers of previously taboo topics—from incest to illness—are now standard fodder for talk shows and television dramas. The message? That *anyone* can fall prey to dark forces.

With all that drama surrounding the dark side, the concept of possible victimization gains ground—and even goes chic, and not just in those repulsive photo spreads of battered-looking models selling couture wear. And it doesn't end with the inexplicable, personal horrors so exhaustively explored in entertainment. Dig a little and you, too, can join the club.

Has free-floating victimhood become a new sort of institution in our culture? Well, maybe it hasn't gone that far. But fears of being done wrong may be more in our faces than ever.

The recent debate over gender issues and children sends this point home. Some experts might argue that girls in our society need special attention because they are at higher risk for low self-esteem, negative body image, poor school performance caused by not wanting to appear "too smart" and other destructive tendencies. These findings have raised hackles of a vocal opposition: boys suffer too, if not more, they say. The heck with Girl Power T-shirts; it's the guys who need more attention, resources, what-have-you.

It boils down to a no-win competition: Who's the bigger victim? With sweeping debates like this, there's a place for everyone. No matter who you are, you can be part of a larger group who feels beleaguered. Of course, this debate, and other Big Umbrage ones like it, raises some important questions. But ultimately, how does it address the needs of children—male or female—who need help, not as a poster children for the issue of gender inequity, but as individuals?

Unfairness abounds, true victimization certainly exists, and debates over who gets the bigger slice of pie in the "at-risk" arena—or any other—will probably continue. The problem with the Group Victim game is that it's a hard place to leave. A sense of powerlessness is unpleasant, but hey, it's home.

So what does this have to do with materialism? Appealing to the victim in all of us is a swell way to sell things, of course—get an object and gain power. And Perpetual Victimhood is a way to *keep* selling things. But ultimately, it may get in the way of shifting from being a victim to becoming a survivor.

Growing Economic Disparities

Who wants to be a millionaire? Doesn't everyone? In recent years, we've heard about new millionaires practically on a daily basis: the tech whiz kid that makes a killing, the winners of an Initial Public Offering Grand Prize, the lucky beneficiaries of some merger or another, along with the usual lottery winners.

In what we now might deem Jackpot Nation, the regular guy gets demigod status when Fortune smiles with piles of dough; we hear about what these people wear, where they live, and how they plan to make their next bundle. They are treated with the same breathless adulation once accorded only to movie stars. Their celebrity, of course, boils down to money, pots of it.

We don't hear so much about those at the other end of the spectrum, the ones now priced out of the places they've lived for years, whose incomes don't match the rising costs of necessities, and who are struggling to simply stay afloat. What's out there but often ignored is the number of people who are poor: According to a recent United Nations Children's Fund Report, 13.5 million (or nearly a quarter) of children in the United States live in poverty, second only to Mexico among industrialized countries.

Because differences in income levels have grown ever-wider, "middle class" may be dwarfed and distorted by Croesus-like standards. Because reversals of fortune now seem to happen with the lightning speed of a game show, anxiety about slipping from the middle—what writer Barbara Ehrenreich called "fear of falling" in the 1980s—seems to be more widespread than ever.

Of course, "survival" is considerably different for a person who worries about how to pay the gas bill than the one who's considering giving up a country club membership. Not long ago, a woman, whose income is in the top 1 percent of this country, told me she felt "poor." "I make okay money," she said. "But I see twenty-somethings making a fortune, and it's unfair. When's it going to be my turn?"

Cry me a river, you might say. Try talking to someone who's trying to raise a couple of kids on minimum wage, and then see if you have anything to whine about. It's hard to summon up sympathy, but then, maybe the woman's entitlement talk is really fear speaking. Fear that she's being shoved off her perch at the top of the heap. Fear that she's too old to compete. Fear that her own idea of "survival" is being threatened.

Maybe you've made more money than you ever thought possible, bought the things you always dreamed of, and find it doesn't deliver what you thought it would. Maybe you worry about losing what you've gained—the higher the climb, the harder the fall. Or maybe you've made a decent living all along but have started to feel like you're now stuck on a rock in a current that seems to sweep ever-onward in monetary and material expectations. Or maybe you've always struggled to make ends meet and that fight is getting tougher. The situations are different—the sense that the party's gonna be over or that the bottom is about to fall out is relative—but the feeling isn't.

For people comfortably above the poverty line, fears about survival, however one defines it, have a way of blocking awareness of good fortune that can't be measured in material or monetary terms. And the endless comparisons with those who have "more" can cloud consciousness and eliminate empathy for those who have less.

Privacy, Purchasing Power, and the Perception of Threats

Imagine the possibility of neighbors prying into your private business by peering into your windows, and multiply it by several thousand inquisitive eyes trained on Windows on computer screens all over. With the advent of the Internet and growing access to medical, financial, and other information, fears about invaded privacy are on the rise. The solution isn't yet clear, but one thing is certain: Polls show growing worries that those bits of data, in the wrong hands, can and will be used against them.

Is Big Brother really watching you, years after *1984?* George Orwell's grim vision of a world governed by Thought Police and the all-seeing, all-knowing eye of the ultraoppressive Big Brother, as set forth in his 1949 novel, has certainly not yet come to pass. But fears that similarly scary pseudo siblings— say, Big Business, Big Insurance Companies, Big Government—can track, in frightening detail, your interests, ailments, purchases, and even, perhaps, your thoughts, as put forward in personal correspondence or records—is of increasing concern.

Interestingly, fears surrounding privacy don't seem to apply to other people's most personal secrets. No longer limited to digging up dirt on old arrest records or surgical enhancements of celebrities, public prurience has reached new levels when it comes to watching the most intimate aspects of other people's lives.

In the 1998 film *The Truman Show*, Jim Carrey compellingly plays Truman Burbank, who has spent his entire life, unbeknownst to him, observed by millions as a character in a television show. As the first baby ever adopted by a corporation, he's existed within the confines of elaborate sets and dozens of hidden cameras; his family and friends are actors who follow scripts, and the dialogue of his "real" life in idyllic, small-town Seahaven even incorporates sponsors' messages. The show's Big Brotherish creators have instilled fears of the outside world in Truman in order to him to keep him there—and keep the show going. It's only by questioning his world and facing his fears that Truman is be able to escape his artificial existence.

The nightmarish quality of the movie—you desperately feel for Truman as he begins to question what's real—comes from both the control of "his" show's creators over his life and his ignorance of just how far he's being manipulated by outside forces. We're interested in Truman's life in a constant, climate- and thought-controlled fishbowl. But we're most interested in finding out if he'll get out of it.

In recent years, the frightening, fictional theme of total lack of privacy has morphed into entertainment *vérité* that purports to be, well, real. MTV's *The Real World*, chronicling diverse groups of strangers living together, paved the way for a wildly popular Dutch television show, aptly titled *Big Brother*, providing twenty-four-hour-a-day access to the lives of willing volunteers. An American version of the show followed.

Is there a connection between fearing invasion of privacy and the desire to do that invading, via one screen or another, oneself? Watching a stranger's every sneeze may not make for scintillating entertainment, but it beats the feeling that some-one's doing surveillance on you. Prurience and privacy con-cerns may go hand in hand.

The more we look into others' lives, the more we may want to ensure that others can't look into ours. We hear the message of "get it before it gets you" so frequently that items such as caller ID, electronic surveillance systems, and computer fire-walls begin to seem essential.

These fears perpetuate themselves, and may continue for years to come: This generation of parents—baby boomers and beyond—is notably fearful, not only about their children's safety and security, but about their future success and prosper-ity. And so we have more "enrichment" programs, more orga-nized kiddie sports leagues, and more must-have toys and edu-cational gadgets for kids than ever. And of course, we can now arm them with beepers and cell phones to be sure they're safe and sound while they're being improved!

The doting doesn't stop with indulgent or ambitious parents or grandparents, either. American children, from toddlers to teens, have emerged as a powerful consumer force themselves. Kids spend more money of their own than ever before (up-wards of $30 billion annually) and exert growing influence on buying decisions on everything from food to cars in their fami-lies. Whether you view it as a smart marketing maneuver or scary manipulation, this new, powerful, and ever-replenishing group—it's never too early to gain brand loyalty—has become more important to reach.

And the reach of this phenomenon has entered new arenas in recent years. In public schools, it has spawned sampling (free candy at lunchtime!) marketing studies during school time (at a New Jersey elementary school, kids completed a twenty-seven-page marketing survey for a cable channel; a preschool in Connecticut had four-year-olds test childproof locks on lighters), math textbooks that amount to ads for particular brands, and numerous new deals in schools that allow companies to monitor kids' Web habits in exchange for technology.

Kids' potential as consumers has made them, now more than ever, the focus of more new magazines, television shows, and movies. And since more than a quarter of our country's teens now have credit cards, it makes sense that they, in particular, rule: Never has the angst of high school, the glamour of early stardom, or the fantasy of having extraspecial powers at an extra young age (say, being a witch, vampire slayer, or transforming creature) been so exhaustively explored. Forget adults knowing anything. Wisdom, in contemporary culture, has the body of a sixteen-year-old and the mind of a thirty-year-old in therapy.

The "build-a-better-baby/child/teen" syndrome of parental involvement these days may include old-time parental fears: Your kids will reject your values; they'll do the same stupid things you did when you were young; your efforts on their behalf aren't enough to keep them safe or make them successful. Coupled with the external focus on kids as consumers—an ever-present message of power without responsibility—it's a daunting combination. If your child truly believes a new computer will help him do schoolwork, it's hard to deny him, even if you can't really afford it.

But perhaps a more crucial element of fear and consuming surrounding kids these days is about protecting them, not only from the outside world, but from themselves and their peers. Footage of school violence is enough to terrify any parent. The idea that no one's child is immune to such attacks takes hold. The fear that any kid could be a killer lingers.

Across the country, that fear has prompted "zero-tolerance" policies regarding violence, any violence. This has led to some interesting interpretations: Kindergartners have been suspended for pointing their fingers in the shape of guns, elementary school children sent home from school for bringing a plastic knife to cut an apple at lunch, and historically accurate cardboard swords kids make for a middle-school project are now confiscated.

As a society on edge from images of real violence surrounding children, objects gain new and sinister meaning: The plastic knife becomes a threat; a cardboard sword is cause for alarm. And yet, as a society enamored of violence-as-entertainment, with kids controlling a big part of culture and consumption—professional wrestling may not be intended for kids, but guess who's watching—something's strange about this picture.

And not a little scary. Obviously, there's a difference between muttering, "I'd like to kill him," and actually doing it. There's a distinction between finger-pointing and real weapons. And a kid who simply likes to dress a little strangely may be worlds apart from another who dresses the same way—and plots to blow up his school. But recent events wrack the nerves, illuminating the possibility of violence everywhere we turn. What's real and what isn't? What's possible—and what's probable? What's form and what's content? And where are the grown-ups who can make calm sense of things? The answers are still out there, and the fears remain, and grow.

Fear motivates: Better safe than sorry. "Security systems" of all sorts—metal detectors, "age-defying" creams, antibacterial soaps, vitamins that "enhance immunity," among others—may help us feel safer, to some extent. But then, there's always the possibility that the metal won't be detected, that aging happens no matter what, that some virus will elude all the soap in the world, and that vitamins don't always provide immunity. We do what we can with objects. But what do they do for an internal sense of security, our real quality of life, or connections to other people?

With images and information on terrifying events—and possible threats—more widespread than ever, it becomes harder to separate the possibility of danger from the probability, to extricate an image on television from one's personal reality. When Americans hear about a shooting, 72 percent worry that it could happen to them or to someone they love, according to a survey. It is easier now to envision the worst.

In an environment that focuses on dangers that may await, distrust may replace faith that people are essentially good. And while the sturdy house of bricks may keep out the wolf, what of the wolf that may be within, the one who remains to strike terror in thought and spirit? Sure, we know rationally that objects themselves cannot build the human connections or optimistic outlook that can help us really feel free from fear—but heck, they can do *something*.

While fear motivates, it may also distract, until we live, like the old Italian saying, with "one eye on the frying pan, the other on the cat." While it can get us to go buy something, fear may also fester in the mind, paralyzing and preoccupying. The idea of potential danger may overwhelm the potential for authenticity, for unity, for empathy. The perceived and real power of possessions to protect may work on many levels. But the sense of security we find in objects may separate us from a deep, internal sense of security in ourselves that helps us feel we can face fear and become free of it, regardless of what life may bring.

Under Siege

The Anglo-Saxon root of the word "fear" means "disaster" or "catastrophe." Through the years, "fear" has taken a step away from an actual event, and entered into the realm of emotion. Fear—along with dread, anxiety, and worry—have come to mean feelings that anticipate or react to possible disaster.

As an instinct, fear warns and prepares us to decide whether to fight or flee, take action or take off, the kind you might imagine happening when a cave lion approached a guy sitting near his cave. What should he do—grab his club and start swinging or run into the cave? What's called the "alarm reaction" is the mental focus and physical preparation we go through in response to possible danger. In a split second, the body and brain prepare us to take action to survive.

While survival now is usually no longer a matter of dealing with cave lions, we continue to have occasional "alarm reactions" ourselves: When a car in front of us on the highway brakes suddenly, do we stop or swerve? Faced with imminent danger, we still react with the "primitive" part of our brains. It's hard to know whether our ancestors who lived in caves worried about *possible* threat when a cave lion was nowhere in sight.

What's certain is that we now think about fears—the concrete disasters of the past—in the future tense. And they probably encompass more possible disasters than ever. Fear includes the "what if?" of anxiety, the possibility of future suffering, the dread of what might happen at some dire, unspecified time. Fear now encompasses myriad surprise attacks—physical, social, emotional—to our survival.

Fear sells. But it can also distort. A woman who decided to stop using credit cards and close her accounts said the first reaction from the companies' customer-service representatives was surprised disbelief. Then, she said, they outlined scary scenarios about what would happen to her if she gave up the card. "What about your credit rating?" they asked her. "How will you rent a car? What if it's your daughter's birthday and you're short on cash?" One representative even asked, "How will you *live*?"

"Since getting into debt with credit cards was ruining my life at the point, the question almost made me laugh. How would I live? I knew I wanted to live within my means, which meant not buying on credit. But all the other fears they brought up hit home, and I even started to question my decision myself. Fortunately, I quickly realized that no matter what they told me, having a card wasn't going to help me deal with my real problem, which was spending money I didn't have."

Fear's power of suggestion is potent. Your credit rating will plummet and you won't be able to buy a house or rent an apartment. You'll be stranded on a desolate highway because you can't rent a car. Your daughter will be terribly let down on her birthday. It's not just a credit card you're giving up, it's your *whole life.*

And it can snowball and expand in the imagination. Aided by advertising, anxiety about public humiliation may grow into an image of a huge crowd of jeering strangers. Worries about your children's safety may place them, in the mind's eye, in an unimaginably horrifying situation. Except that with the imagination, all is possible.

Since we continually hear about the possible worst-case scenario—from personal humiliation to global devastation—the "it could happen to you" may morph into "it will happen to you, if you don't do something." Of course, the power to "do something," generally means purchasing or consuming something. Avoiding humiliation becomes a matter of using the right antiperspirant, avoiding danger means buying something—or thousands of them—that promises protection.

A few summers ago, a thirteen-year-old from Norway spent several weeks with an American family. She seemed to be having a good time, except for one thing: She never wanted to go out by herself, not even to take a walk around their quiet suburban neighborhood. Knowing that she was quite independent at home, they finally asked why. She was afraid of getting shot, she said. The American television shows she saw—along with the news she heard—made it seem like you couldn't be safe anywhere in this country. And she wasn't taking any chances.

Most of us don't take what we see on TV so literally, but exposure to multiple images of murder, mayhem, and medical emergencies infiltrate our consciousness at some level. We're forced to acknowledge the possibility of bad things happening, and potential powerlessness in a terrible situation. But we have the power to put them into perspective. It's possible to turn "what if?" into "what's probable?" focusing on our own reality-based experience, as opposed to images we see.

The Limited Good

The catastrophic earthquake that happens many thousands of miles away can produce anxiety, but it's the smaller ones striking closer to home that may rock our worlds more. What we have in comparison to those in other countries may be interesting, but what we have in comparison to those who live on our block may be more meaningful. In a culture that looks ever upward in achieving safety through material means, the danger of getting caught in a landslide looms ever-present.

As a psychologist I interviewed said, "Nobody in this country reflects on how far they've come, only on where they're going." So what if you don't happen to be movin' on up? You may be sunk.

Physical dangers are one thing. Given the emphasis on social security through objects that abounds in our culture, social dangers are equally meaningful. The wrong brand of jeans, we hear, could send a preteen straight to social Siberia.

An interesting element to the message that objects offer "insurance" against disasters of all sorts is its temporality: The policy keeps changing. The must-have jeans of last year are dork-wear this season. The lifeline is available for a limited time only.

So we may worry that we might not get our share of "the good things in life." Imagine a bag of candy to be divided among a bunch of hungry children: If someone else gets a piece, there's one less piece for you. Now, imagine that bag contains all good, desirable things—luck, money, health, for example. If something wonderful happens for your neighbor, it's one less good thing out there in the universe for you. Anthropologist Oscar Lewis and others called this outlook "the image of the limited good." Although originally used to describe "primitive" cultures, the idea of "limited good" is alive and well in the world's richest country today.

How often do we hear that something for sale is so special, such a deal, and in such short supply that we'll be shut out if we don't act fast? "Only 500 available—when they're gone, they're gone forever!" may not strike terror in your heart, but it creates an incentive. Clearly, the last thing these messages seek to promote is mindfulness; the quicker the connection between wanting something and laying down cash, the better. Spend now for a rainy day: These exhortations imply you're somehow endangered until you take possession of something. Safety arrives only in ownership.

But safe from what, exactly? Possessions promise all kinds of protection, but the pitch of limited good with objects boils down to a pretty simple premise: winners and losers. Winners are safe, happy, and have something—tangible or not—worth protecting. Losers are everyone else.

Remember "Mystery Date," an old board game for girls? Created in a prefeminist era, the idea of the game was not to amass property as in Monopoly, or to catch a killer, à la "Clue." The object was to snag a man.

Not just any man, mind you. You could end up with "The Dud," an unkempt, oafish guy whose mere presence would cause death by embarrassment at the Sweet Shoppe. Winning the game meant a date with the blandly handsome, clean-cut young fellow who would presumably sweep a lucky young lady off to a lifetime of security. (Of course, this was in the long-ago days when we didn't worry about Mr. Dreamboat turning out to be Ted Bundy, and it was long before Dud look-alikes ended up running Silicon Valley software companies.)

"Mystery Date" may seem ridiculously old-fashioned these days, but the "winner take all" message hasn't really changed very much. Consider the Melanie's Mall toy collection, where tiny teen Melanie and her friends come complete with their own gold credit cards to buy things at stores (each sold separately!) with names like Beauty World and Glamour Gowns.

Needless to say, the play set doesn't come with Boring Dolores, who abstains from spending because she's pushed her credit limit a wee bit too far, or Slick Rick the Repo Man, or Judge Janice of Bankruptcy Court. Winning means acquisition.

And this message isn't just for kids. How many times have you heard about products that offer a "competitive edge," or give you something you can "count on"? Do you use paper towels you can "trust"? If not, you may be at risk.

The accoutrements of safety—from physical to social to spiritual protection—have gone from the realm of the dull and cautious to multipurpose status symbols. Divine protection comes in the luxury car that claims it "can not only help save your life, it can help save your soul as well." The security system's sticker outside houses proclaims that your house is worth protecting. (The message isn't just for criminals!) And what could be safer than upscale logos that appear, not just as a relevant afterthought, but throughout the very fabric of an object?

Fear, says a character in the Albert Brooks comedy *Defending Your Life*, is "like a giant fog" that blocks happiness and joy. The movie takes place in fabulous, fictional "Judgment City," where each soul has the opportunity to stand up for his or her life after death. There, Judgment Day isn't a reckoning of sins or good deeds, but how you handled fear on Earth. The people who overcame fears in living get to move on to a higher level of being; scaredy-cats and cowards must return to Earth to try again.

The judgment in that fictional city may not exist, but there's something to the idea that fear can get in the way of getting what we want most. And while it may not be a "giant fog" in our lives, it may impede clarity. How, in an anxiety-filled environment, do we move beyond fear itself?

Internal Security

Fear itself—what Franklin D. Roosevelt identified in 1933 as a "nameless, unreasoning, unjustified terror which paralyzes needed efforts to convert retreat into advance"—has gotten many names, given myriad reasons, and become justified through a plethora of images and information inconceivable when he made his inaugural speech. But it is no less paralyzing now than in the past. How do we change retreat into fear into advancement of growth, and, well, joy?

One approach, which a woman I know uses with her children as well as with herself, is to get a handle on small fears by asking questions: What's the worst thing that could happen? And then what? And what next? Will your life be ruined if you don't buy the backpack everyone else has? What would you still have if the worst happened?

There's probably no final answer to the question of confronting fear, but finding a personal plan, rather than purchasing another product, may be a start. Fear may be a messenger, offering an opportunity for personal growth. And while it may prey upon our feelings of powerlessness, it also offers an opportunity for realistic assessment of what we can and can't control.

Another woman mentioned that the first lines of the Serenity Prayer, written by the theologian and social activist Reinhold Niebuhr, helps provide her with a reality check on fear. It may now be the stuff of greeting cards, but it makes sense. The prayer asks for "serenity to accept the things I cannot change, courage to change the things I can, and wisdom to know the difference." The materialized framework insists that control and change is possible through purchasing. The "spiritual" approach accepts both the limitations and possibilities of change, the price—and benefit—of which is courage, conscious serenity, and wisdom. And perhaps now more than ever, some of each approach may be necessary to feel less fearful.

Working on what we can actually do to feel less afraid requires considerably more time and energy than buying a quick, impermanent solution: Actually practicing a speech before you need to make it, however, is more likely to ensure success than simply using the antiperspirant. Installing another set of locks can certainly help keep out the bad guys, but developing relationships with neighbors may help us feel less alone against them, easing worry and mistrust. Challenging ourselves to change, through effort, the vision of the worst-case future to one where everything comes out all right isn't easy, particularly in the current environment. But building on an internal sense of strength about what we can do, not buy, what we can be, not be victim to, may be a small first step toward serenity.

We live in a culture that constantly promotes the idea of limited good alongside images of unlimited evil. And that's just how it is. But if we want to feel less fearful, we need to turn the equation around—to cultivate a sense of good that is limitless. What doesn't run out or expire? Pleasure gained from others' good fortune. Opportunities for experience. A sense of trust and security with other people and yourself that transcends locks and keys. And perhaps awareness, not of what might get taken away, but of what we have.

10

❧

CONTROL

The thrill was in the trying on, in the buying.
The moment after she had acquired something new
it became meaningless to her.

—JUDITH KRANTZ, *SCRUPLES*

Here's the deal in the story: He'll get the power to have whatever he wants, whenever he wants it, in exchange for something he alone possesses. The thing he has is one-of-a-kind, irreplaceable once it's gone. But imagine, complete control in your life! It's tempting, no?

If you're familiar with Goethe's *Faust*, you probably know that the bargain-maker is the devil, and the item up for trade is a human soul. Oh yeah—there's a bit of proverbial fine print in the contract that Faust overlooks at first. Sure, he can control anything. However, that doesn't mean he'll ever feel satisfied. And that's the hellish problem here: Without his soul, Faust is perpetually dissatisfied, not matter how much he gets.

Okay, so maybe most of us wouldn't sell our souls for total control, but there can be days when it might seem like a fair trade. While it's pretty obvious that nobody can achieve perfect control over every aspect—or even just a few aspects—of life, the impulse to try is there.

We may not be power-mad control freaks, but taking charge of how we live now and in the future can certainly aid us in becoming happier. And even if you don't own a crystal ball that offers amazing insight into present and future, possessions can and do remove some of the disorder from daily life—and offer some control.

Control at cut rates is especially enticing. The tagline of the trendy, cheap clothing store that says it's "where shopping is fun again!" hits on a widespread motivator among both men and women: more than 85 percent of both sexes cite price as an important factor in where they shop. Along with price, being treated with respect and a "low-pressure" environment are priorities for consumers. Just as in the early 1900s, when Charles Coolidge Parker did some of the earliest studies on department stores and proclaimed "the customer is king!" we still want to rule for a day—or at least for the time we spend shopping. When acquiring objects, we want to feel in control.

Shopping has always been fun, of course, but it goes beyond that. While the experience of purchasing may vary from culture to culture—the long tradition of good-natured haggling between buyer and seller in an open-air market is a long way from dashing into the superstore to grab something from a bin—the act of acquisition provides an opportunity to take charge. Think about it: Does any other cultural experience offer the thrill of the hunt with few dangers, a game where you determine the outcome, and most important, a feeling of control?

Unlike dealing with your less-than-perfect family or that pompous client or annoying colleague, the act of shopping is appealing because it's so uncomplicated. You can't return the colicky baby, but you can return the booties that don't fit. You can't easily swap your spouse for a more suitable one, but you can get the jacket that works in exchange for the one that doesn't. And while there's no way to get around certain things—such as the time it takes to grow, the energy involved in building relationships—shopping offers the possibility of a bargain, the path of getting something you want for less via the sale rack.

Even if you don't happen to find what you're looking for, the activity is inherently democratic. And possibly, it's empowering. You might not have the money for the new car, but you can take it for a test drive. You may not need the new hat, but you can try it on for size. You're free to look; you can even take something home and see how it fits into your house and still be under "no obligation." And when your world may be out of whack, when circumstances spin out of control, shopping provides an opportunity to take your mind away momentarily, to stimulate the senses. It enables you to find and possess at least one thing that, well, fits.

And let's face it: It can work, to some extent. Obviously, you can't control other people's decisions regarding most other things in life, but the choice to part with money for something is all yours. While shopping may not quite live up to the messages that equate the activity with the ultimate in free will—hey, the piper has to get paid somehow—purchasing power is real, whether it's a kid spending baby-sitting money on candy or an executive forking over a year-end bonus for a new motorcycle.

Although the act of shopping may offer simple temporary control, our expectations of objects we buy can get a lot more complex. And the temporary control may crumble.

A group that helps people get out of debt has two ways of categorizing out-of-control consumers: underearners and overspenders. The underearners simply don't make enough money to sustain their purchases; they buy things they have to have, they say, but come up short financially each month. Or as a physician with three home equity loans put it, "I just have to start making more money, and then I'll be fine."

The overspenders habitually live beyond their means, and if one were to take a nineteenth-century view of revolving debt or buying "on time"—once considered somewhat shameful, since you were supposed to "save up" for something you couldn't afford with cash—the group would now include a huge segment of our population. The underearners, too, are stretched to the limit and often beyond. Do they really need what they buy? Does it matter?

Other than semantics, the main distinction between underearners and overspenders may be one of self-perception. Both spend too much money. Both feel the need to get the problem under control. For underearners, the answer is in making more money, pumping up earnings to support spending habits. For overspenders, the goal is to spend less, not necessarily earn more. On two sides of the same coin, so to speak, the problem is debt and money.

But where does the money go? The approach here—and perhaps, throughout our culture—is that buying stuff is an immovable, near-natural force. Control over debt becomes control over the amount of money you can spend, not necessarily thinking about why you feel you need to buy something. And so "controlling" debt becomes a matter of "just" making more money—hey, no problem, in theory—or spending less on what you're buying.

Since consumption is essential to surviving, the issue gets tricky. However, when buying more objects gets positioned as an uncontrollable constant, it takes on the quality of, say, dealing with a downpour. You have two choices: You can buy a cheap umbrella or an expensive one, now that you have that second job. Seeking shelter elsewhere isn't an option in this setup. So where does real control lie?

The Rise of OOCs

A few years ago, I read somewhere about "OOCs," an acronym for people who felt Out Of Control with the multiple demands and desires in their lives. Although the shorthand didn't catch on the way "yuppie" had a few years earlier, it summed up a sense of the center not quite holding. And as a current leitmotiv, it's caught on fast.

Why, at a time when we can control more than ever before—imagine ear infections before antibiotics, winter without gas or electricity, life without telephones—does a nagging sense of being off-kilter persist? Of course, we can't control everything: A hurricane happens even if you *have* spent months rebuilding the house from the last storm or planning the beach vacation. Still, since we can now use objects to control so much, that old chestnut about money may apply: Feeling in control, like feeling rich, is having just a little bit more than what you've got.

The symbiotic relationship between objects and feeling in control has been around forever, but the rapidly expanded—

and real—power of objects to handle the once-unmanageable may affect our perceptions of what we can actually control, and what we can't. The reply of buying to get things under control may make us feel more intent on having to get a grip, more disgruntled when the control doesn't come—and more overwhelmed than ever.

Obviously, objects don't control us. But in recent years, the place where control lies may be increasingly linked to getting and spending. How come?

Time and the calendar of consumption.   We waste it, spend it, pass it, save it, juggle it, and try to stop it. Time can't really be a controlled substance, since it comes and goes regardless of what we do. But our concept of time may be more controlled by consumption than ever.

Forget following seasons by watching leaves change color or seeing the first crocus come up: We live at a time when Halloween costumes appear in stores in the heat of July and Christmas decorations surface before Halloween even happens. As a result, we may end up living in at least two "time zones." There's the one where you can feel the snap in the air, smell the snow coming, or see the buds on the branches. And then there's the one where you're perpetually behind in what you are supposed to buy. Now you can begin to feel things are out of control—months ahead of schedule!

While the lag between "buy time" and real time has increasingly gotten out of whack in recent years, it's been decades since consumption first became a driving force in our calendar. In the early 1900s, a woman named Anna Jarvis sought to establish a holiday honoring mothers. By 1914, the second Sunday in May became an official national holiday. But all was not victorious for Jarvis: By 1923, infuriated by the commercialization of Mother's Day, she fumed, "This is not what I intended. I wanted it to be a day of sentiment, not profit!" Shortly before her death in 1984, (when the extent of honoring Mom could be measured by whether you sent her a bunch of roses, a nightgown, or—ooh la la!—a jeweled watch) Jarvis even told a reporter that she was sorry she'd ever started Mother's Day.

It's still up for debate whether Father's Day (think belts, ties, shirts, and electronic gadgets) was actually invented by a greeting-card company to double the profits of honoring parents, but clearly, consumption has played into our national time frame of annual events for a while. New Year's Day and the Fourth of July haven't yet changed to suit retail schedules, but the day of Thanksgiving—perhaps our most important national holiday of all—shifted specifically to promote consumption. In 1939, a prominent retailer convinced President Roosevelt to move the holiday from the last Thursday in the month to the fourth, with the idea that a longer Christmas shopping season would boost the economy.

With the U.S. economy still struggling to recover from the Great Depression, the idea wasn't entirely unreasonable. And while conspiracy theorists might argue that our conception of time is now controlled purely by some dark and mysterious corporate-profit motive, why bother? What's worth noting is that the now-skewed time frame of consumption—moving further and further from "real" time—may contribute, more than ever, to people feeling out of control.

Climate control and the cult of comfort. "I'm just not comfortable with that right now," said my eight-year-old. I'd just told him to go do his homework. He wanted to continue reading a comic book. It's a minor point of pride that I resisted the urge to say something snide. Instead, I ignored his comment about comfort and repeated that he needed to do his spelling. Mumbling that I was mean, he went off and did it.

Even among eight-year-olds, the cult of comfort has come into common parlance: Why bother to do something necessary if it's "uncomfortable"? Climate control through comfort is a current theme in consumption. (And it transcends jogging suits passing for acceptable dining attire.)

The comfort-over-all ethos asks us questions: Who, after all, would don plain old snow boots to shovel out the driveway when you could be wearing a footwear system suitable for sub-zero yak-tracking in Tibet? Why risk driving a little old car to the beach when you could be controlling the kind of military vehicle that did time in Desert Storm? Then again, why not be the first on the list for the ultimate-in-comfort, coming-some-day "concept" vans that feature microwave ovens, entertainment systems, washing machines and dryers and more cupholders than a small airplane?

To be swaddled in luxurious fibers; to bask, fetus-like, in a big, squashy chair surround-sounded by your home-entertainment system; to be cosseted (with the implication of an attractive flight attendant tucking you in with a bottle) on your next transatlantic trip—the images and messages that sell comfort these days presume a desire to be treated like a large baby. Warm fuzzies in the form of objects reproduce at a rapid clip: Think of heated leather car seats, kitchens the size of single-family homes, and toilet tissue infused with fragrance and moisturizer to make the most of your bathroom experience.

Okay, there's a reason that stiff, spiky horsehair sofas are no longer too popular, and frankly, there's much to be said for those toasty car seats on cold winter days. And while squishy-bodied pens don't necessarily produce great work on their own, they feel nice in your hand. The stuff of comfort can add a little pleasure to the day, even if you're not inclined to want to be "babied."

Still, the current comfort hoopla blurs lines. Physical comfort gets intertwined with emotional and spiritual peace: Not only does the makeup look and feel good on your face, it "nourishes" the spirit, too, we hear. "Climate control" communicates control of other things.

But let's examine the body-mind-spirit connection here. Sure, your family can sprawl better in the kitchen with overstuffed couches, and the professional-quality oven may mean the turkey and pie can cook at the same time, thus avoiding the discomfort of waiting. The space-age refrigerator can produce enough ice so that no one has to suffer a lukewarm soda. But while the house can be filled with the comforting smells of Thanksgiving dinner, is that any guarantee that anyone will actually want to be there? Or feel thankful?

Since comfort counts for so much these days, discomfort has taken on dark overtones. Feeling "uncomfortable" is vague and ominous, connoting that something is terribly wrong, or could be. It suggests that something is out of control.

Feeling "uncomfortable" may be legitimate, or an excuse, however flimsy, for choosing not to do something. But because the promise of comfort control may merge with emotional, intellectual and spiritual control, all may seem possible, with the right down pillow or ergonomic keyboard. And perhaps, when doing away with discomfort of one kind doesn't magically produce the sort of control we seek, it's back to the drawing board. Or to the next product promising comfort—and control.

The Pitch of Pain

The comfort ideal reverses the old idea that suffering is good for the soul: Salvation is no longer found in donning a hair shirt, but in buying one crafted from three-ply cashmere. "No pain, no gain" might still be a motto in high-school locker rooms, but in just about every other setting, pain is something that should always be avoided—and can be, if you buy something.

Like the drone of a mosquito buzzing somewhere near your ear but always slightly out of reach, the pitch of pain is ever-present in our culture. And it's all presented at the same frequency. From the "heartbreak" of psoriasis to the angst of spotty dishes, from the distress-filled "sinking feeling" that dinner will be late getting on the table to the suffering of "social anxiety," we are bombarded with messages pitching pain avoidance. Heart disease, halitosis, and hair loss get equal billing. Disappointment, embarrassment, annoyance, boredom, or anything that intrudes on delirious happiness or undiluted comfort becomes a crisis.

Chances are that it won't destroy your day if the dishes have a couple of spots, but with all possible afflictions identified in the same way, suffering gets magnified. Like the fairy-tale Princess and the Pea—only a real princess would be sensitive enough to feel a pea through a hundred mattresses, never mind that it's kind of rude to mention it to your hosts—fixable suffering may even become a distinction.

Even though she's faked the whole thing, the princess in the story gets the ultimate reward: She becomes queen. And suffers no painful repercussions, like, say, getting caught in her lie and banished from the kingdom forever.

The story neatly sidesteps the issue of side effects. Contemporary pain relief may produce some unexpected results, not only limited to the hair-loss treatment that may cause impotency or aggression when you regain that full head of hair. And it isn't just medical products that have side effects: Buying the big house may relieve the pain of living in a cramped apartment, but problems between people often continue and may grow, no matter how vast or comfortable their home. Here's the problem: When objects simply can't control pain, it may return, worse, perhaps, than ever.

Does doing away with spotty dishes provide a remedy for what Buddhists call *dukkha*, the suffering of human existence? As multipurpose pain-relievers for mind, spirit and body, objects purport to heal any hurt, do away with discomfort, and stop pain in its tracks, no matter how deep or diffuse. So— where *does* it hurt? Despite the number of messages we receive about the win-win of pain relief and obliteration, there's something to be said for examining what pain, exactly, we're trying to control.

Pain is unpleasant, inconvenient, a drag. Suffering stinks, and discomfort is no barrel of monkeys, either. Still, there may be something to the Buddhist idea of joyfully participating in the sorrows of the world. Radical though it may sound in the current culture, there may be something gained from accepting pain.

At around the time he communicated not feeling "comfortable" about having to do his homework, my son complained of mysterious, fleeting aches and pains. He wasn't sick or injured; the pediatrician could find nothing wrong. "Growing pains," was the off-the-cuff diagnosis, something I remembered experiencing in my own childhood.

The old-fashioned expression "growing pains" seems like an oxymoron in an environment that continually presents growth as acquisition and pain as something to be controlled by consuming. But, obviously, going through something painful is sometimes necessary to get to eventual pleasure: Copying spelling words is a pain, but it enables you to be literate later. And as the philosopher Epicurus observed a couple of thousand years ago, dealing with pain in the present may mean eliminating far greater suffering in the future. Hey, growing pains hurt, but consider the alternative.

In the current climate of consumption, no pain/all gain is a potent, recurring message. Still, it's worth considering the idea that pain control through objects may, in fact, perpetuate rather than relieve it. And while feeling "comfortable" is certainly desirable, it's also worth exploring the idea that controlled comfort doesn't necessarily diminish pain—or ultimately, give us what we want.

Although not all pain control works as an anesthetic, it tends to be an approach our culture has embraced on many levels. We use more drugs than ever to take the edge off a myriad of less than perfect moods (Martin Seligman, as head of the American Psychological Association, once called depression in

the United States an "epidemic"), have more "extreme" entertainment to take us away from our own, perhaps dull, lives, and
have more ways to purchase something that may not relieve
pain, but distracts and puts a temporary damper on it. Don't
look and it won't hurt, is the promise.

But what if the pain remains? An elementary school teacher
tells me the contemporary approach is to leave spelling, math,
and grammatical errors uncorrected, because corrections can
be painful for students. Since pain has gotten both so frightening and seemingly controllable, a secondary-school administra-
tor says he sees more adolescents who have never been allowed
to experience pain or even disappointment—and fall apart
when they finally encounter it.

Sure, ignorance may be bliss to some. A friend of mine owns
a cat who fell on her head as a kitten—and purrs incessantly,
even when she gets a shot. And while never seeing a correction,
never experiencing lows or highs may work for some, it may be
like running on pain killers: It can also cripple. And perhaps,
deaden feeling for longer than you'd like.

But back to pain and growth. It's worth questioning the current "anesthetic" approach to controling all emotional and
physical pain and entertain another idea: While feeling pain
may hurt, it can also heal. And it's worth examining whether
"aestheticizing" emotional or spiritual pain—allowing yourself
the time and focus to feel it, experience it, accept it—may, in
fact, be a lasting way to feel some control over it.

A midwife once described the pain of labor as a "difficult
friend" to me. Golly—that wouldn't be the first analogy that
most mothers I know would use. Still, it's interesting to consider. While difficult friends can be intense and hurtful at

times, one who's close doesn't lie. While difficult friends may cause suffering, they deliver equal—if not more—parts of pleasure. Difficult friends aren't always pleasant, and you can't control what they do, but one thing is certain: They're friends because they also give so much. The difficult friend of labor, said the midwife, may bring the worst pain of your life—and the greatest miracle.

Okay, this isn't intended to be a pitch for natural childbirth, or express anything but admiration for the widespread availability of, say, epidurals. But it is a way of looking at pain that runs counter to materialized wisdom: *acknowledging that experiencing life involves experiencing pain.*

The phoenix is the mythical bird that achieves immortality, renewing its youth by bursting into flame and burning alive. It's certainly not a pleasant image. But then, actually growing in real life sometimes requires sitting in a kind of metaphoric fire for a time.

Of course, unlike the phoenix, we've got to keep scrabbling through. On the other hand, while pain may recur, it doesn't last for eternity, either. Countering the notion of pain relief through objects may involve accepting that we can't always control pain any more than the phoenix can extinguish its fire—but knowing that it probably won't last forever, and we may grow from it, whether we buy something or not.

Revisiting Control

At around six P.M. one evening many years ago, a journalist from the *New York Times* approached several people in a city supermarket. Would they like to have Pierre Franey, the venerable food writer, cook dinner in their homes that evening? The deal was this: he would use only ingredients already in the person's cart and home kitchen at the time he approached them.

Now, if you know anything about Pierre Franey, this was akin to a French culinary fairy godfather showing up in real life. Instead of having to think about and prepare dinner after a long day, Mr. Foodie himself would come home with you and perform his magic while you relaxed! Three lucky people enthusiastically said yes.

The results were mixed, some comical. According to the story, a young man, whose cart contained a slice of watermelon, carrots and a bag of chips, and whose kitchen yielded little more than an old head of garlic and box of pasta, ended up eating Mr. Franey's spaghetti, carrots and fruit balls for dinner. He called the meal "wonderful!" and added: "The one thing Pierre and I have in common is that he takes whatever he has got and puts it in."

These days, would anyone open their doors to a stranger—no matter how strong the press credentials—who wanted to give a whirl to "making do" with already-there ingredients in their homes? Safety issues aside, the risks involved with creating something out of what you already have—no matter how skilled the chef—is one that runs counter to control-through-acquisition. Forget making "x" out of "y," and never mind that cheery concept of making lemonade out of the lemons: Now we hear about the choice between frozen concentrate, "fresh" in a carton, powder that you mix up with water, sugarless or not, and so on. While we probably don't want to give up the control that comes with choice, it's worth looking at the lemons—or carrots in the cart, so to speak—and examining control in another way.

Despite the choices we have in lemonade or anything else, what's out there may still not be just right. So perhaps it's worth relinquishing the idea of control through objects in order to gain it elsewhere.

Of course, freedom isn't always "just another word for nothing left to lose," in the old words of Kris Kristofferson. Still, actual control may mean recognizing opportunities in what already exists, instead of seeking control in the next acquisition. Look at it this way—dinner may be awful whether you take the potluck approach or buy every ingredient on the list, but it may be wonderful, too. So loosening expectations might help us feel more free. But it can also help, paradoxically, to help us feel more in control. If dinner doesn't always have to be a culinary masterpiece, it's a lovely surprise when it actually is. If you don't insist on being in complete control at all times, what a pleasure it becomes when something works just right.

Accepting that the unpredictable and uncontrollable are simply part of life may lend control. And recognizing that forces beyond our control can actually contribute to life may help make us happier.

Nearly a hundred years ago, the Swiss psychiatrist Carl Jung came up with the concept of "synchronicity" to describe meaningful coincidences—seemingly unconnected events that provide insight or understanding. Is it sheer coincidence that you dreamed of an old friend, overslept and missed the plane you were supposed to catch the next day—and then ran into your friend at the airport? Is it simply odd luck that you're not hired for a job you want—and end up, and hour later, getting a call out of the blue for one you want a lot more?

Were these situations "meant to be" or something more random? It's hard to know. The point of considering synchronicity is that it may provide some context for control. Obviously, these events aren't connected by straight cause-and-effect, but through individuals making connections to make the coincidences meaningful. And maybe control can come through perception—certain events are beyond our control, but how we choose to interpret them isn't.

In an environment where control is constantly connected to consumption, the idea of synchronicity may rank right out there with superstitions surrounding black cats and broken mirrors. In an age of Mars exploration, earthly "meaningful coincidence" may seem, well, ludicrous. But perhaps now more than ever, it's worth considering not just what we can and can't control, but how. The connections we forge, the meanings we bring, may be the only true control we have.

Connecting to Control

Benjamin Franklin once proposed the wild turkey as our national bird. The large, rather ungainly creature was beaten out by the bald eagle, of course, but the story doesn't stop there. Once plentiful throughout the country, wild turkeys were over-hunted to the extent that they became extinct throughout New England and much of the Middle West by the 1920s. It seemed a sad fate for a near-national symbol, a grand and allegedly clever creature—not to be confused with the dim-witted domesticated type of turkey—that had played such a prominent role in our nation's history.

But all was not lost. About forty years ago, wildlife groups across the country began to adopt initiatives to bring back the bird, with astounding success. In Connecticut, for example, conservationists released twenty-two turkeys in 1975; today, they number around 30,000. Across the country, the wild turkey population is now about three million, a hundred times what it was at the end of World War II.

So what does this little conservation lesson have to do with control? Certainly, the story is a triumph of control, where efforts to reverse what once appeared to be inevitable extinction paid off. But beyond that, the impressive, nearly four-foot-tall birds that now occasionally stalk through my backyard signify something else: a connection to what the naturalist John McPhee calls "deep time."

I'm no turkey expert or naturalist, but there's something remarkable in considering that the birds I now see outside are descendants of a mere twenty-two released little more than a quarter century ago. And that those twenty-two are connected to others in the past, and so on, until you get back to a time, unimaginably distant, when the birds, resembling reptiles, had no name.

But they are connected to those I see now. Just as my son comes home from school bursting with the news that the raindrops we feel on our faces may have once fallen on George Washington or even a cave dweller, there's a link. The vastness of time, the immensity of connection through living things, isn't always in mind, say, when you're a suburbanite watching deer eat your tulips or an apartment-dweller who spots a cockroach. But it's there.

In everyday life, pondering deep time may give way to dealing with those darned deer who are munching your garden, the uninvited cockroach in your kitchen, or the rodent who's happy sharing a home with you. And apart from those mundane distractions, the materialism-driven messages we hear so frequently don't exactly assist us in thinking about anything older than yesterday's paper.

In fact, the materialized approach to time usually gets about as deep as "whoever has the most things when he dies, wins." So what's the prize? Objects can't control or stop time, of course. The ongoing connection to the deep past and the distant future that simply *is* in living may continue to some extent through possessions—sure, we uncover ancient pottery shards, and no doubt someone several thousand years from now will find meaning in the detritus of our own time—but that link is limited to a tiny dot in an infinite scheme. What of a million years from now? Or ten?

Connections to possessions *can* make us feel in control in the present. Still, it's worth examining them in another way by considering the idea that objects aren't "owned" as much as "lent" to us during our lifetimes. And that what we actually own now—and what really endures—is a collection of genetic material, and how we choose to treat ourselves and other people.

The power of viewing control as an intricate series of connections, rather than serial consumption, is that it may remove a large burden from our lives. Instead of having to be masters of the universe, it's possible to simply feel part of it.

11

Dematerializing

For the beginning is assuredly
the end—since we know nothing, pure
and simple, beyond
our own complexities.

—William Carlos Williams, "Paterson"

Martha Stewart once wrote an article for the *New York Times Magazine* about why she was leaving Westport, Connecticut, the town where she'd lived for nearly thirty years, growing her business from a small catering concern into a media empire. She said she'd "tried to ignore the warning signs" of what made her unhappy in the town and took action in her own home: She completely redecorated her house, rearranged cupboards, enlarged her gardens, and added a couple of new kittens and some chinchillas to her collection of pets. Still, Stewart wrote, she'd come to the conclusion that the town "just doesn't work for me any longer."

Why? Although she focused on a specific small town, her complaints about heavier traffic, large, impersonal chains replacing small-town stores and service, and the rise in big fences and decline in neighborly relationships over the last thirty years could have been about almost anywhere. Then again, was it those environmental changes—or was it her? Either way, she touchingly wrote about feeling isolated and lonely, "no longer connected to the neighborhood."

In response, letters to local papers poured in for weeks: Although some supported Stewart and her criticism of the town, many amounted to an outpouring of bile suitable to a terrible sort of betrayal. And the message of several letters was a simple, nasty "good riddance." Okay, the article wasn't exactly a puff piece on the place, but why would so many people respond with such venom?

Perhaps it was Stewart's honest note of defeat, her admission that attempts to create real change with a "new and beautiful palette of colors," "carefully edited" furniture, or more animals in the menagerie wasn't enough. Coming from the country's best-known creator of "gracious living" through lovely objects, the world's most successful purveyor of purchasable perfection, the message might have struck a particularly raw nerve for some. Martha, say it ain't so, the letters seemed to say. You aren't just disrespecting the town—you've become a traitor to the cause of consumerism! How could you?

Like Scarlett O'Hara raising the old, inedible radish to proclaim she'll never be hungry again, at the end of the article, Martha rallied. "I'm confident that the move will be excellent," she briskly announced. But where did that leave the true believers? Writing angry letters, perhaps.

Wherever you go, the old saying goes, there you are. Of course places change over three decades, whether we like it or not. People change, regardless of fresh paint or new pets. But whether it's a town or a house or a car—or even a person—that no longer works positively in your life, it doesn't take a creative genius to know it's still *you* seeking something else. And when the "it" of acquisition doesn't work any more, when the place where you live, so to speak, doesn't feel like home any longer, where do you go?

Big events have a way of forcing us to look inside the place where we actually live, offering perspective. Anyone who has ever loved someone who is seriously ill knows it's impossible to obsess over needing new golf clubs at that time in your life. The lost earring becomes absurdly unimportant when you've lost someone. In the face of true adversity, material minutia that can occupy so much of our lives, time, and energy stop meaning so much. What really matters becomes clear.

The wake-up call of a bad event puts what's important—and not—in its place. But what about the rest of the time? Messages equating changing curtains (or anything else) with changing your life aren't going to stop. The tide of materialism will keep coming in. And while dematerializing may happen because of a bad event, why wait? It may be impossible to alter consumer culture, but it's possible to take some small steps *now* to gain perspective by retrieving power from the messages of possession-obsession. Which might begin with a simple premise: To change your life, think about changing your mind.

It doesn't take much. Here are some ways:

Consider that three out of four's not so bad.   A few years back, I was complaining to a neighbor about the hot, muggy stretch of weather we were having. The air felt so heavy you could hardly breathe. You couldn't walk a block without getting sweaty. It sapped your energy. And so on. I was going on and on about horrible heat, and my neighbor agreed it was hot, but didn't join me in my whining. Jokingly, I asked if she enjoyed 95-degree weather with staggering levels of humidity. She laughed and said that she didn't. But, as she put it, "I think people should only be allowed to complain about one season. So I save it all up for winter, which I really hate."

Now, this was an interesting idea. Complaints can feed on themselves—the worse something seems, the worse something else seems, and so on. Call it negative energy, if you wish. Or a sure way to put the damper on enjoyment. In either case, complaints can multiply, merge into each other, and become a way of viewing the world, and what you don't have. Okay, we know it can't be 78 degrees and sunny every single day of the year. But when we decide it *should* be, the "winter of our discontent" can last all year-round.

Only saints and martyrs can avoid complaining completely. But limiting yourself to one season—and deciding that you can put up with the other three—seems like a sensible idea, a principle that could be applied elsewhere.

Certainly, some things merit objections. But it's possible to pick battles. It's possible to decide that three out of four things we whine or gnash our teeth about aren't really worth the effort or energy, and that, perhaps, withholding complaints may be a way of actually seeing something to enjoy.

Okay, so maybe it *was* hot and sticky. But my neighbor was right, I decided. Winter's worse.

Turn swords into plowshares.   The word "toxic" has come into use in recent years to describe not only objects that may be poisonous, but people as well. A person who is "toxic" is a bit like hazardous waste—dangerous, destructive, and unpredictable.

It's a powerful way to objectify people. Toxicity implies a fast-acting poison with few antidotes, an attack from which there is no escape, a power—nearly magical—that one person has over another. And it implies powerlessness on the part of the person who's the recipient of "toxic" behavior—unless you're on guard to defend yourself.

While we may not be surrounded by toxic people, everyone has to deal with others who are less-than-ideal companions or colleagues. Everyone has experienced a blindside attack of one sort or another. And although they may not make us feel literally poisoned, they may not improve the qualities of our lives too much, either.

Objects may come into play in both attack and defense with destructive people. So here's an idea: Instead of viewing their behavior as a toxin, view it as a sword that may be turned into a plowshare for your own benefit.

Alex, a man who'd recently been laid off from work, described a tactless attack from another man who knew he was experiencing hard financial times. At a party, the man started talking about the elaborate boat he was going to buy. Then he launched into a detailed description of building an addition on his house. The toxic zinger came when he commented on Alex's "cute little place" and asked if they were ever going to move. And by the way, how was the job hunt going?

Alex was ready to walk, but a stranger standing near them came to the rescue. She starting asking about the boat, why he liked to sail, and so forth. And, said Alex, "It turned out his wife hates sailing, and this guy has some fantasy of going off for months at a time—he even mentioned living full-time on the boat by himself—while his wife lives alone in that big house. I thought, what a sad way to live, and he was bragging about it! The guy's a jerk, but he told me more than he probably wanted me to know. And he made me realize that I'd take a small house and a decent relationship any day over planning my future around buying a way to get away from my wife."

When it comes to object-based, toxic attacks that make you feel inadequate, consider the source. The attack may sound personal, but then again, you just may have been the available target for their arrows of bitterness at the time. And keep in mind: Withdrawal of emotional investment doesn't mean defeated retreat. It means putting the emotions elsewhere, where they matter more.

Clear out.   Does having fewer things make your life less complicated? Of course that depends on the things—and the person. Getting rid of excess stuff can certainly make your house more orderly, and finding another home for an object that you no longer need or use can make you feel good.

This is why the practice of "simplifying" by exchanging, say, ten different outfits for a few basic mix-and-match pieces is so appealing. Still, you may *like* having the ten—or fifty—outfits. And while that one, simple, Zen-inspired arrangement may look lovely on the mantelpiece, it doesn't necessarily do away with the desire to deck the halls with lots of glittery stuff a month later.

Nor should it. The point here is that a current focus on material "simplifying" doesn't necessarily address complexity of desire. Or as one woman put it, "it swaps one form of consumption for another. It seems to be about style, not substance." Even if you embrace the "less is more" adage for a while, you may still find the closets of desire are packed full again before you know it.

So perhaps one way to actually clear away the excess is to examine its impact on your life. And be honest with yourself: Why are you holding onto something? Do you still need it? Do you still want it? Will you run out and buy something else just like it if you get rid of it? Will you still want, want, want? Bringing mindfulness to the process of getting rid of things—or holding onto them—may not make life more simple. But it may help us get a handle on our own complexity, and help us decide what's worth keeping. As one woman said,

> In my fourth move in four years, when I was packing up my grandmother's six sets of dessert plates once again, I knew I'd never used any of them, ever. It hit me that I didn't even like most of them very much, couldn't put them in the dishwasher, and had felt obligated to keep them so I would remember her. But I didn't get anything out of having them. When I sat down and thought about it, I realized that I would remember my grandmother with those plates or without. And I was happier getting rid of them instead of hauling them to another house.

What do you actually get out of having something? What would you miss in letting it go? How would you benefit? Asking these questions may not help your life get any simpler, but it may offer understanding into what you want to keep—or not.

Dematerialize deprivation.   There are people in the world who don't have enough to eat. There are people in the world who don't have a place to live. There are people in the world who have no family, no friends, nobody to turn to. There are people who live every day with true deprivation.

We may know all these things rationally, but amid thousands of messages urging us to spend more, consume more, *want* more, the reality of the situation becomes a little like parents prodding kids to clean their plates because there are starving children somewhere else in the world. A disconnect occurs: It's hard to forge a link between your own act of wasting food and someone else receiving it a million miles away. Especially when most of what we hear about deprivation tends to focus, not on those less fortunate, but on what we ourselves are missing.

When we compare the deprivation that we may feel because we don't have some object or another to the deprivation of, say, not getting essential nutrition, our own concerns can seem pretty petty. Definitions of where the "poverty line" falls vary, but a demographer I spoke with says it's often presented as a proportion: If your entire income is more than three times what you spend on food, you're living above the poverty line. Which doesn't allow a lot of leeway for, say, rent, utilities or clothing. Or paying a doctor's bill.

Although thinking about real poverty may help us get a grip on how much we have by comparison, it doesn't necessarily make a personal sense of deprivation go away. So what does? Perhaps dematerializing deprivation means considering what is actually making you feel deprived. Even if you realize your reasoning may be a little silly, the feeling may be real. Accepting that feeling, and acknowledging that a sense of deprivation may be inevitable at times—you can't always get what you want, but you get what you need, as the song goes—may help put what you don't have in perspective.

And it's worth examining the concept of relative poverty and wealth. Aided by our environment, poverty consciousness can hit the wealthy as well as those truly in need. In the same way, feeling "rich" may not have a lot to do with your bank balance. As a woman who was one of six children raised on a postal worker's salary put it, "It was a huge treat for all of us to go to McDonald's, but I never, ever felt poor when I was growing up. We talked a lot about how much we had." Regardless of circumstances, it's worth considering this: What makes you feel rich?

Several years ago, a man I interviewed said he consciously began giving away a dollar a day to people who begged in his city neighborhood. "I've heard arguments against giving money to people on the street. But if I can give one person a little money that might make the difference between being hungry and not, why shouldn't I help? It may help them, and it helps me feel rich to give something away."

A final word on deprivation and those people in the world who have so little: Giving to others may not diminish your own feelings of deprivation, but it can't hurt, either. Your donation of money or time can't completely do away with others' deprivation, but it may contribute something to another person's life, which, in turn, may contribute to your own.

Discover the intrinsic.   A friend once told me that her nine-year-old was complaining because they didn't have a basketball hoop in their driveway. He wouldn't do well in team tryouts, he

said, because "everybody else" in their suburb had a paved driveway and a hoop to practice on. A couple of kids even had those
expensive basketball shoes that made you jump higher, he told
her. He'd never make a good team, he whined.

Instead of arguing that she regularly took him to a nearby
park to play, or delivering a pep talk on self-esteem, his mother
took a different approach: "You can't buy tall," she told him.

It stopped the child midsentence. He looked down at his
large feet and up at his mother. And smiled. "I *am* tall. And you
can't buy that," he agreed.

I liked this story because the mother didn't talk to the child
about "someday" when they could afford to pave the driveway
or buy the shoes. She didn't deny his desire or worries by
telling him to pipe down. She dealt with reality, focusing on
what he had right then, and would never, ever be able to buy:
height. And she gave him a gift in helping him to see it.

In Betty Smith's *A Tree Grows in Brooklyn*, an ambitious,
impoverished mother yearns to give her children more. But she
also weighs what they have: "My Neeley has a hole in his. . . cap
and it's stretched out of shape but he has thick, deep golden
hair that curls. My Francie wears no hair bow but her hair is
long and shining. Can money buy things like that? No. That
means there must be something bigger than money." Her observations go beyond the external: Her daughter is a "learner,"
and "there is music" in her son. She begins to plan for her children's future by acknowledging who they are—that can't be
bought—in the present.

Although the book takes place at the turn of the century, the
point holds true today. Our kids may now grow up in an environment where very little seems "bigger than money" and what

it can buy, but clearly, being a "learner" or tall aren't purchasable, and probably never will be. It takes a little effort to remind yourself—and help remind children—of the things that simply, intrinsically *are*, and are good. But seeking out and celebrating the things that are larger than purchasing power may ultimately help us—and our kids—feel more complete.

Question screen time.   The average American spends twenty hours or more a week watching TV. Throw in the growing amount of time that people spend on-line, and playing video games, and it adds up to the fact that many people in our country spend a major portion of their lives in front of one screen or another.

Screen time has been blamed for everything from physical problems to declining intellectual abilities, moral laxity and even depravity, and praised for everything from its educational value to opening a window on the world for more people than any other medium in the history of man. Since screens give us access to entertainment and information with unprecedented ease and variety, we're probably not about to get unplugged, despite some of the possible downsides. There's no question that television-watching and Internet use are a mixed bag. But more to the point, it's clear screens are an important part of our culture, and will continue to be.

It doesn't take a media expert to figure out that time spent in front of screens is time not spent elsewhere. And while increasingly affordable technology allows more people access to television programming and the Internet than ever, it's worth considering that expenditure of time, and the possible price it may exact in other areas of our lives.

"Free" TV or premium service, "unlimited" Internet access or not, commercial messages are now part of life, like it or not. Since media is a business, reasonably enough, nearly *all* screen time is now "pay per view," even when it's free. So what's the currency demanded of us in the exchange? Time, of course. Attention. And a possible leasehold on desire.

Now, this is not to say that it's feasible or desirable to blow up your TV or throw out your computer. It's not to say that either medium turns people into unthinking, ever-unsatisfied automatons. But here's the point: It's worth considering how screen time contributes to material desire. It's worth becoming more mindful of background noise and how it may affect what we believe. And it's worth considering that a conscious effort to cut, say, a half hour a week from screen time may provide a way to devote both time and attention to something more important.

Sleep on it.   Do you want something? Do you really, really want something? What is it that you actually want?

Throughout history, people have used dreams to understand themselves, other people, and events, along with giving insight into the future. Call it an interplay of subconscious desires— think of Freud's and others' work. Or look at it as "journeying" with spirit guides, like the "primitive" native people of southern New England and many others, who believed people had two souls: the immortal "dream soul," which left the body during sleep and illness to seek enlightenment, and the "clear soul," that lived in the heart. Either way, it's widely believed that sleep can inform and illuminate. And it may offer some insight into what we really want when it comes to objects—or other desires.

To "sleep on" a big decision, especially one that involves buying, is an old-fashioned idea, one that isn't highly prized in an era of instant credit and limited time. But it's worth trying. Writing down a question about what you want before you go to sleep is no guarantee that you'll have an answer in the morning, but it does allow your mind to move away from the immediacy of the object and mull over what you're actually seeking.

Reinstitute a day of rest.   If sleeping on a decision is an old idea, here's one so ancient it's positively new again: a day of rest.

Blue laws, which were first established in this country in 1781 and prohibited shops from operating on Sunday, are, for the most part, a thing of the past. Some towns, counties, and states still bar the sale of alcohol on Sundays, but we now have the option of acquiring nearly anything else round-the-clock. It's a godsend for many busy people, but it makes it tough to *ever* remove ourselves from a pattern of wanting and consuming. To counter the increasing importance of having something to show for our time, it's worth revisiting the concept of a day of rest.

What does rest—call it downtime or even idleness—*do* for you? As opposed to "recreation" or "leisure" time, it may allow you to disengage from advancement, achievement, and acquisition and give you the opportunity to contemplate the "given." of what's there. For one day—or even half a day, or just an hour—each week, removing oneself from the obligation to fix or improve may help sharpen the focus on cherishing what *is*.

We get a lot of prompts about "getting away from it all," from the bubble bath that claims to take you elsewhere to the (corporately sponsored) quarterback who shouts, "I'm going to Disney World!" in response to the question of what he's going to do after the big win. But why not consider something more regular that doesn't depend on "wins" or "losses" during the week? A conscious day of rest isn't about getting away so much as getting in touch by savoring what's here, now.

Create a will for living.   I once heard about a strategy to figure out your life in twenty minutes or less: Write your own obituary. What would you like someone to say about you once you're gone? What accomplishments would you like to see enumerated?

Now, this exercise seemed like a swell idea until I started thinking about it a little. An obit may be a neat summary, but then, unlike Huck Finn and Tom Sawyer attending their own funeral, it's unlikely you'll ever get to hear your own eulogy. And then there's the problem of time, space, and details. An obituary may list your prizes or public discoveries, but it can't really include the tiny triumphs or private discoveries. It can't list the small acts of heroism or simply soldiering through—say, the number of diapers you uncomplainingly changed or the endless meetings you sat through without losing your mind or temper. Finally, there's the problem of timing: Hey, when your obituary finally appears for real, you're *dead*. Are you really going to care what anyone says about you at that point?

A woman once told me that she had everything together in her life—her house was nice, her car was nice, her job was nice. The only thing she was lacking, she said, was her life's work.

Since I'd never stopped to think about the idea of "life's work," this brought me up short. And it made me come back to the idea of obituaries, which, if you're looking for an external summary of someone's life, isn't a bad place to start. But if you'd rather try to find a life's work rather than its summary, maybe a "will for living" is a better place to begin.

Considering one's "will" or purpose in living—not some grand scheme or vaunted accomplishments that get noted at the end of a life, but those that might be found in the process of being alive—may be more useful than the short summary of a fantasy obituary. Maybe another way of trying to find one's life's work is to consider this: *Living* is one's life's work. This is it—no second drafts or reruns allowed.

Shopping, among other things, offers an experience. And objects, to some extent, enable self-expression. Still, at the end of the day—or life—what's there, really?

So possibly, instead of sitting down and writing that imaginary obit, it's worth thinking about your own will in living— what you value, what you want, what you've got. And what, perhaps, you'd like others to inherit from the time you spent on earth.

Reexamine excess.   Tall, grande, "super size"—whatever happened to a small, or even a "regular" cup of joe? We live in an era punctuated by the embracing of extremes, in everything from more challenging, daring, or violent sports to the growing size of cars or houses to over-the-top luxury (*luxe populi* for

all!) associated with high-priced items. So what's "excessive"—
and what isn't?

Since desire isn't just based on "need," it's hard to sort out.
And because we're not about to get any guidance on this front
from the external wisdom of our culture, it's something to consider in our own lives.

Discussions of materialism have a long history of considering
how people connect to objects. Does the worker feel a connection to what he produces? Does the consumer feel a connection to a brand?

Perhaps one way to reexamine the idea of "excess" is to consider some connections: The size of the car or house, the resources it uses, and the impact on the environment and so on
are a start. But equally meaningful is the personal connection—is it too much, too little, or just right? Why? When it
comes to objects, we regularly hear echoes of Mae West's sentiment that too much of a good thing is wonderful. Let's face it,
though—she wasn't talking about the size of sodas at 7-11. So
what's worth having in excess—and what's not?

Work with living things.   On a ferry a few summers ago, I noticed a curious phenomenon: A great number of the women on
the boat (including me) sported similar necklaces. Well, they
weren't exactly necklaces—they were "virtual pets" strung on
cords around our necks. They were the toy-of-the-moment at
that time, entrusted to us by our children.

Perhaps "entrusted" is the wrong word. It was more like "in-
flicted." You see, the toys needed regular attention. By pressing
buttons, you could "feed" the little LCD picture of a creature,
clean it up, play with it, even it teach it to do tricks. If you

didn't, it would "die," heaven forbid. The three-hour ferry trip was punctuated by the darned beeping of the electronic toys demanding something, along with rueful, knowing glances exchanged by the mothers who ended up having to deal with the stupid things.

Okay, the toys had the advantage of being marginally less trouble than, say, a puppy. But in retrospect, there was something strange about the scene on the boat. So much anxiety and a sense of, well, responsibility to an LCD display. So constant. And ultimately, so unfulfilling, both for the kids who insisted on getting the toy in the first place, and for the parents who ended up with the things. Talk about a virtual albatross around your neck.

The virtual pets came and went in a flash: After the initial excitement, they became, well, a bore. Which might be said for many of the "virtual" experiences objects promise.

While the virtual pet craze didn't convince me to get a real puppy, it made me start thinking about living things. And why working with them may be helpful in dealing with a materialism-driven culture.

It isn't just that my kids got more out of scooping up starfish on the beach and "saving" them by throwing them back in the water than they did in all the weeks we toted around that annoying toy. The point is that living things may offer satisfactions in unpredictability, wonder in the unique, and connectivity and responsiveness that can't be acquired in an object.

The toy may have made its owners feel "needed"—indeed, it was touted as a wonderful tool to teach responsibility. (Just who actually felt "responsible" became clear on that boat, of course.) But here's the glitch: It would never do anything that wasn't preprogrammed. It was unsatisfyingly limited, and had some alarming results: Driven to distraction by the demands and diminishing emotional returns from the things, perfectly nice, normal children I knew eventually started performing euthanasia on their virtual pets.

Living things, on the other hand, respond, provide surprises in just being, and deliver something that's difficult to find elsewhere. And what they give may help us shift perspective away from the ever-present focus on "more" satisfaction through objects.

Consider yourself lucky.   A friend once told me a story that some might consider blasphemous, but then, maybe not. When she was a child, her mother was seriously ill, and her father sent her and her brother and sister to attend Mass on Christmas Eve while he stayed at home to care for the mother. The three kids were feeling very low—their mother was so sick, they weren't in the mood to go to church, and the prospect of Christmas the next day seemed pretty bleak. The three children had spent many happy hours in movie theaters during that bad time, and more than anything, they wanted to go to the movies instead of going to church.

Of course, religious or moral questions aside, they had no money for the movies. As she glumly walked toward church, something caught my friend's eye on the slushy sidewalk. It was a crisp, new twenty-dollar bill.

Okay, they could have gone to Mass, put it on the collection plate, and felt grimly virtuous. Or they could do what they did: See it as a miracle. Accept the gift, wherever it came from. And take the money and celebrate Christmas Eve in an unorthodox way at the movie theater.

Was it dumb luck, or a divine sign? Was it a random occurrence, or was someone or something looking out for those kids? Who knows? The point is that it meant something to my friend, who told me this story twenty years later. She and her brother and sister got just what they needed and wanted. And they saw themselves as incredibly, amazingly lucky that night.

With the "pull-yourself-up-by-your-own-bootstraps" history and myth of our country, luck is often presented as solely something you make for yourself. You hear that the power of chance is a looming, negative force—take charge or lose out. And that message, of course, is paired with something you can buy to produce the desired outcome.

Sure, you *can* make your own luck. Still, who can explain fortuitous events that sometimes just happen? Considering yourself lucky may not necessarily change your luck, but it may alter the impact of materialized messages you receive so frequently. Recognizing good luck where you can won't change what you hear—but it may change how you respond.

Seek the spark.   In India, a common greeting that translates loosely as "I see the divine spark in you," is offered to strangers and loved ones alike. It may just be a pleasantry, along the lines of our own use of a "God bless you" when someone sneezes. But it's also worth considering the sentiment more carefully.

Through more ways than ever these days, we hear stories about strangers that have little to do with "spark," divine or otherwise. More frequently, we hear that masses of Others are our competitors, our betters, our predators—and we'd better protect ourselves from them with an object.

Now, maybe we wouldn't call every guy we run into on the street "divine," but the idea of a spark inside that unites people is an interesting idea. The possibility of seeing that spark, of recognizing the potential for goodness in a person—not in what they wear or drive—is intriguing. Sure, the spark may not grow into anything greater. But it might. And we don't know until we look.

That spark is what is real, what is authentic in all of us. Not the "authentic" jeans we purchase or the "real" off-road vehicles we drive. The spark is the absolute, not our possessions. The "inner knowing" of authenticity, the "trueness to thine own self," may be dissected and distorted through promises of the "real." So what's at your core? What's whole? What's authentic? What's your spark?

In an essay on running a marathon, Julie Curtis-Ames wrote about hearing her five-year-old son discuss her accomplishment with a classmate. The classmate asked if she won the race, and her son said no. "So what's the big deal, anyway?" the other kid taunted. Her son's response? " 'The big deal,' he calmly stated, 'is that she started.' "

Which could well be applied to the process of challenging a possession-obsessed culture. The races will still be run, the medals will still matter, and the messages of various all-or-nothing "big deals," no doubt, will continue. But in dematerializing them—by questioning what we really want and need in our own hearts—we may start to find what matters more. We may begin to discover what's not enough. And what is.

Recommended Reading

The Nicomachean Ethics by Aristotle (translated by J. E. C. Welldon, Amherst, New York: Prometheus, 1987) In one of the earliest explorations of what constitutes "the good life," the Greek philosopher examines the nature of happiness, virtue, wealth, and material goods. Aristotle's lively opinions on these issues—which he put forth more than 2,000 years ago—remain relevant and interesting.

The Theory of the Leisure Class: An Economic Study of Institutions by Thorstein Veblen (New York: Modern Library, 1934). First published in 1899, Veblen's classic, often cantankerous, and sometimes-amusing study of status and consumption is worth another read more than a hundred years later. Although some details of objects—and what constitutes status—may have changed a bit since his day, his sharp observations of both "conspicuous consumption" and "conspicuous waste" in turn-of-the-century America still shed light on consumer motivation and buying behavior today.

Democracy in America by Alexis de Tocqueville (translated by Henry Reeve, with an introduction by John Stuart Mill, New York: Shocken, 1974). In 1831, the young French aristocrat

Alexis de Toqueville came to America to study the country's penitentiary system; he ended up examining its people and political systems, publishing this volume in 1834. Hugely popular in Europe when they were published, Tocqueville's critical, sometimes-admiring observations of American democracy continue to provoke thought.

Walden; Or, Life in the Woods by Henry David Thoreau (New York: New American Library, 1980). Thoreau's "experiment" of leaving his home in Concord, Massachusetts, to spend two years in a humble cabin on Walden Pond produced what is surely the most famous, oft-quoted volume about living a "life of simplicity." His contemplations about contemporary life—the book was published in 1854—and finding spirituality in nature are eloquent, passionate, and inspirational.

The Lonely Crowd: A Study of the Changing American Character by David Riesman, with Nathan Glazer and Reuel Denney (Garden City, New York: Doubleday Anchor, 1953; a new revised 2001 edition is now available). In the middle of the twentieth century, sociologists Riesman, Glazer, and Denney set out to explore the differences in "social character" between Americans of the 1950s and their predecessors. The result is this still-engaging book, which contrasts the differences between "inner-directed" Americans of the past with "other-directed" tendencies in modern life. Although the research here is from the late 1940s, the "modern" character the authors discuss is still recognizable.

Man and His Symbols by Carl Gustav Jung and M. L. von Franz, Joseph L. Henderson, Jolande Jacobi, and Aniela Jaffé (New York: Dell, 1968). Produced by the great psychologist and four of his closest followers shortly before his death, this book was intended to explain some of Jung's theories on the relationship between the unconscious and conscious mind to the "average reader." Jung's ideas on the relevance of dreams and myths, and his concept of synchronicity or "meaningful coincidence," are among the subjects explored here. Another source for further reading on synchronicity is Jung's *Synchronicity: An Acausal Connecting Principle* (translated by R. F. C. Hull; edited by G. Adler; Princeton, New Jersey: Princeton University Press, 1973).

The Culture of Narcissism: American Life in an Age of Diminishing Expectations by Christopher Lasch (New York: W. W. Norton, 1978). One might argue, more than twenty years after Lasch first published this well-researched, well-written book on "diminishing expectations," that we live in an era of *heightened* expectations, especially when it comes to material objects. No matter. Lasch's keen observations on the impact and importance of image, "pseudo-self-awareness," and promises of consumption in contemporary life, among other subjects, still make for intriguing reading.

The Overspent American: Upscaling, Downshifting, and the New Consumer by Juliet B. Schor (New York: Basic Books, 1998.) Through extensive research, the author of *The Overworked American* explores spending-as-social-act in this excellent book, making a compelling case for voluntarily "downshifting" from over-the-top consumption. Schor, an economist, participated in and included results from the 1995 Merck Family Fund poll on Americans' views on consumption, materialism, and the environment, which is also worth a look. You can find it online at http:www.iisd.ca/linkages/consume/harwoood.html.

Culture Jam: The Uncooling of America by Kalle Lasn (New York: Eagle Brook/William Morrow, 1999.) The Vancouver-based founder of *Adbusters* magazine offers a strong critique of American advertising and consumer culture and its impact on life—and ideas for activism so that you, too, can "jam" these influences. You may not agree with everything Lasn espouses, but his clever, passionate writing gives a fresh perspective. (After reading this book, you may never look at commercials in quite the same way again.) Equally thought-provoking is *Adbusters* magazine and its Web site: www.adbusters.org.

Consuming Desires: Consumption, Culture, and the Pursuit of Happiness edited by Roger Rosenblatt (Washington, D.C.: Island Press, 1999). This diverse collection of essays by a variety of social critics explores various aspects of American consumption, including its environmental, social, and emotional impact.

Your Money or Your Life: Transforming Your Relationship with Money and Achieving Financial Independence by Joe Dominguez and Vicki Robin (New York: Penguin USA, 1999). First published in the early 1990s, this best-selling book, recently updated, continues to offer practical ideas on gaining perspective on personal finance. Exploring how much "life energy" goes into making and spending money, the authors outline a nine-step process to help readers get out of debt, slow down the getting-spending cycle, and make values-based purchasing decisions. Leaders in the voluntary simplicity movement, the authors founded the New Road Map Foundation, a nonprofit organization that promotes "service as a route to personal health and social revitalization" with a focus on personal finances, health, and human relations. Their Web site can be found at www.newroadmap.org.

Both *Quick Fixes and Small Comforts: How Every Woman Can Resist those Irresistible Urges* by Georgia Witkin (New York: Villard, 1988) and *Women Who Shop Too Much: Overcoming the Urge to Splurge* by Carolyn Wesson (New York: St. Martin's, 1990) offer insight into why "shopping until you drop" may be so appealing—and possibly, so destructive—to women, along with practical advice on curbing buying urges.

When All You've Ever Wanted Isn't Enough: The Search for a Life that Matters by Harold Kushner (New York: Pocket Books, 1987). Rabbi Harold Kushner offers a compassionate, theology-based exploration of finding more meaning and fulfillment in life.

Flow: The Psychology of Optimal Experience by Mihaly Csikszentmihalyi (New York: Harper Perennial, 1991). How can we enhance the quality of our lives? In this very readable book, psychologist Mihaly Csikszentmihalyi delves into the concept of engaging in focused "flow" as a means to developing greater satisfaction in what we do. Using his own extensive research and anecdotes, Csikszentmihalyi explores how people can control their own consciousness to experience deep enjoyment.

Mindfulness by Ellen J. Langer. (Reading, Mass.: Addison-Wesley, 1989). With fascinating, scientific grounding, Ellen J. Langer, a Harvard professor of psychology, explores how we may become mindless in everyday life, and offers insight into developing conscious mindfulness by changing attitudes and behavior in this useful, readable book.

Blindness by José Saramago (translated from the Portuguese by Giovanni Pontiero, New York: Harcourt Brace, 1998). This novel, whose author won the Nobel Prize in literature in 1998, is a parable: What would happen if nearly everyone in your world rapidly went blind? Contemplative, beautifully written and disturbing, this novel provokes thought about the material world— and the nature of knowing, seeing, and human relationships.

Index